bare•

MW01233298

Number 7   **Summer 2021**

Editors
Peter Enfantino
John Scoleri

Layout
John Scoleri

Writers
Stephen R. Bissette
Matthew R. Bradley
J. Charles Burwell
Peter Enfantino
Kim Newman
William Schoell
David J. Schow
John Scoleri
Duane Swierczynski
S. Craig Zahler

Artist
Ken Mitchroney

*bare•*bones thanks
Paula Ford
Vonna Gissler

This issue is dedicated to
Marilyn Eastman
(1933 - 2021)
and
Charlie Watts
(1941 - 2021)

Read more online at:
barebonesez.blogspot.com

Cimarron Street logo by
Martin C. Walsh

Table of Contents

2 **Dueling Editorials**

3 **The Stuart Gordon H.P. Lovecraft Adaptations** by Matthew R. Bradley

13 **Once Upon a Time . . . at the New Beverly** by Duane Swierczynski

17 *Once Upon a Time in Hollywood* — **A Roundtable Discussion on Quentin Tarantino's novel** with Stephen R. Bissette, Kim Newman, David J. Schow, John Scoleri and Duane Swierczynski

49 **Genre Film Comic Adaptations** by William Schoell

61 **James McKimmey: The Dell First Editions** by J. Charles Burwell

79 **Digging Into Crime Digests** by Peter Enfantino

87 **S. Craig Zahler on . . . Pulps!**

91 **Sleaze Alley** by Peter Enfantino

99 **R&D: See the Movie; Buy the Book** by David J. Schow

106 **About the Contributors**

*bare•*bones is published by
Cimarron Street Books
Santa Clara, CA 95050
cimarronstreetbooks.com

© 2021 Peter Enfantino & John Scoleri

ISBN: 979-854104-639-7

Wholesale inquiries contact: CimarronStreetBooks@gmail.com

DUELING EDITORIALS

Of all the theme issues we ran in our *Scream Factory* days, my favorite was on the "dark suspense" genre that was all the rage at the time. In that issue, we also devoted space to the "old timers"; writers such as Jim Thompson, Gil Brewer, John D. MacDonald, and Bruno Fischer. But there are so many more crime writers that time has forgotten.

One of those writers is James McKimmey, an author who was relatively forgotten until Stark House began reprinting the writer's novels. In this issue, J. Charles Burwell does a deep dissection on McKimmey's essential Dell First Editions in what I hope will be the first in a series of pieces designed to give you pause and have a second look through that two-dollar pile at the book show. As a bonus, I ride Burwell's coattails with a look at McKimmey's short fiction for *Mike Shayne Mystery Magazine*. In the future, look for spotlights on William Ard, Stuart James, Harold Daniels, and John Burton Thompson. And we do take suggestions!

The award-winning director and author S. Craig Zahler returns with a look at some of his favorite pulpsmiths and stories, and I was lucky enough to read four very strong Greenleafs for Sleaze Alley this time out.

All in all, this could very well be our Best Issue Ever!! Until next time, at least.

Peter Enfantino
Gilbert, AZ
August 2021

Welcome to the latest issue of *bare•bones*!

While retaining our eclectic mix of contents, you may notice that there is a thematic thread running through this issue — that of adaptations. The translation of content from one medium to another, a topic often of interest to fans of fiction and film. And one you'll regularly find us returning to between our covers.

This time out, Matthew R. Bradley provides a look at Stuart Gordon's wild H.P. Lovecraft adaptations, William Schoell explores the comic book adaptations of dozens of genre classics, David J. Schow explores the world of film and TV novelizations, and we're pleased to bring you an epic roundtable review of Quentin Tarantino's novelization of his 9th film, ***Once Upon a Time in Hollywood***. We're particularly excited that this feature brings with it several heavy-hitters to the pages of *bare•bones*: Stephen R. Bissette, Kim Newman and Duane Swierczynski.

We hope this is just the first of many times that you will see their names listed on our masthead. Duane already has a few surprises in the works, and in this issue he also provides an event report on the book launch of Tarantino's novel held at the New Beverly Cinema in Hollywood.

Also making his *bare•bones* debut in this issue is artist Ken Mitchroney, who provided regular cartoons for David J. Schow's Raving & Drooling column when it appeared in *Fangoria*. We're thrilled to have Kenny serving in the same capacity for us!

Finally, I want to take a moment to wish my co-editor Peter a very happy 60th Birthday! As recounted in our introduction to **The Best of The Scream Factory**, he dragged me into this publishing game more than 30 years ago, which means we've been at it for more than half of his life (and nearly all of mine!). There's little we haven't experienced in that time: births, deaths, loves and losses — not to mention that one time he felt the need to freak us all out by having a heart attack! He's my older brother from another mother (and I know I can annoy him as only a younger brother can). I couldn't have asked for a better partner for this wild ride, so if you enjoy *bare•bones*, be sure to raise a glass to the man without whom we wouldn't be here. Cheers, Peter!

John Scoleri
Santa Clara, CA
August 2021

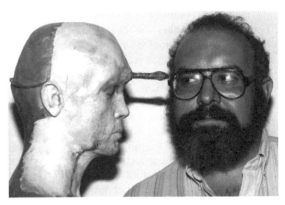

ALL YOU NEED IS LOVECRAFT
The Stuart Gordon Adaptations
by Matthew R. Bradley

After a theatrical career in Chicago, helping to establish playwright David Mamet, the late Stuart Gordon (b. 1947) burst onto the cinematic scene with his very first feature, the audacious H.P. Lovecraft adaptation *Re-Animator* (1985). Its success led to a follow-up, *From Beyond* (1986), and over the years he became — as Roger Corman had with Edgar Allan Poe — Lovecraft's most frequent screen interpreter. Gordon's other official HPL adaptations are *Dagon* (2001) and the *Masters of Horror* episode "Dreams in the Witch-House" (11/4/05), although *Castle Freak* (1995) is said to draw partly on a pair of *Weird Tales* offerings, "The Outsider" (April 1926) and "The Rats in the Walls" (March 1924).

Originally serialized in the February-July 1922 issues of the amateur publication *Home Brew*, "Herbert West — Reanimator" is notable as the first appearance of HPL's fictional Miskatonic University. Later reprinted in *Weird Tales* (March 1942-November 1943), and collected in the Arkham House volume **Beyond the Wall of Sleep** (1943), the six-part tale is narrated by the recently disappeared West's friend and former assistant. He relates the events of more than 17 years earlier, in their third year at Miskatonic's Medical School in HPL's Arkham, Massachusetts; there, West "had already made himself notorious through his wild theories on the nature of death and the possibility of overcoming it artificially."

Part one, "From the Dark," notes that he had been "debarred from future experiments" by the dean, Dr. Allan Halsey; forced to attempt their "calculated chemical action" in secret, he and the nameless narrator occupy "the deserted Chapman farmhouse beyond Meadow Hill," and unearth a fresh drowning victim from the potter's field. This "brawny young workman" is at first unresponsive, so they go into the lab to adjust their formula, only to hear an "appalling and daemoniac succession of cries . . . " They leap out the window, later learning from the newspaper that a lamp they upset had burned the place to ashes, and the grave they refilled had been disturbed "as if by futile and spadeless clawing at the earth."

A year later, in "The Plague-Daemon," West and the narrator, now with their degrees, are pressed into service as typhoid, which the selfless Halsey treats heroically, hits Arkham. Moonlighting in the dissecting-room, West tries a modified solution on an insufficiently fresh body, which merely "opened its eyes [and] stared at the ceiling with a look of soul-petrifying horror before collapsing . . . " Worked to death, Halsey is revived by West, who mutters, "Damn it, it wasn't *quite* fresh enough!"; mauling the medics, the revenant flees through West's window, ravaging Arkham with a cannibalistic murder spree before being captured and incarcerated at Sefton Asylum, whence he has escaped in a "recent mishap."

"Six Shots by Midnight" are fired by West into his newest subject, Buck Robinson, "The Harlem Smoke," whose death in an illegal boxing match supplied no-questions-asked raw material. The duo has set up as general practitioners in Bolton, a nearby factory town, in "a rather run-down cottage near the end of Pond Street," convenient to the potter's field, where in a secret lab they continue tinkering with the solution. Another seeming failure, the body was buried in the woods, only to turn up rattling West's back door, the hand of a missing child (whose mother, an Italian peasant, hysterically succumbed to a weak heart, for which her husband blamed West, pulling a stiletto on him) clutched between its teeth.

HPL's description of Buck bolsters charges of racism: "He was a loathsome, gorilla-like thing, with abnormally long arms which I could not help calling fore legs, and a face that conjured up thoughts of unspeakable Congo secrets and tom-tom poundings [!] under an eerie moon." In July 1910, in "The Scream of the Dead," their problem remains that "the least decay hopelessly damaged the brain structure, [requiring] bodies from which vitality had only just departed . . . " Enter Robert Leavitt of St. Louis, opportunely *sans* family; his own heart gives out en route to the Bolton Worsted Mills, and his body is kept fresh with "embalming compound" until West's assistant returns from visiting his parents in Illinois.

West's long-sought goal, "a rekindled spark of reason," is achieved, if briefly, as Leavitt revives just long enough to cry, "Help! Keep off, you cursed little tow-head fiend — keep that damned needle away from me!" In March 1915, in "The Horror from the Shadows," our storyteller is "a physician with the rank of First Lieutenant in a Canadian regiment in Flanders," having followed Dr. West, now a "celebrated Boston surgical specialist," into enlistment to seek raw material. He has grown to fear West, whose "zeal for prolonging life had subtly degenerated into a mere morbid and ghoulish curiosity . . . His interest [had become] a hellish and perverse addiction to the repellently and fiendishly abnormal . . . "

Now reanimating detached body parts, West seeks to learn "whether any kind of ethereal, intangible relation" links them, and "whether any amount of consciousness . . . be possible without the brain . . . " To this end, he cultivates "never-dying, artificially nourished tissue obtained from the nearly hatched eggs of an indescribable tropical reptile," a covered vat of which he keeps bubbling in the dark corner of his lab in a field hospital at St. Eloi. His new subject, Major Sir Eric Moreland Clapham-Lee, D.S.O., literally drops from the sky, nearly decapitated in a crashed plane piloted by now-unrecognizable Lt. Ronald Hill; a sometime student in secret of West's, the surgeon was ironically on his way to join them.

West places the head in the vat, patches up the body, and injects his solution, whereupon it waves its arms, groping blindly in an apparent effort to escape the airplane; just before a German shell destroys the building, seemingly survived only by West and his assistant, they hear a voice cry, "Jump, Ronald, for God's sake, jump!" . . . emanating from the vat.

"The Tomb-Legions," the last episode, is set in Boston a year after West's disappearance, as the narrator recalls his growing fear that some of his subjects besides Halsey may yet survive, and perhaps even seek vengeance. West made "shuddering conjectures about the possible actions of a headless physician with the power of reanimating the dead," he says.

His fear is justified, for Halsey is liberated in a deadly raid on Sefton by silent, automata-like men and a wax-faced figure "whose voice seemed almost ventriloquially connected with an immense black case he carried." Soon after, a two-foot-square box is delivered, addressed by Clapham-Lee to West, who elects to incinerate it unopened in his sub-cellar lab, but as they do so, a "grotesquely heterogeneous" horde opens an aperture in the wall of a secret chamber underneath the ancient cemetery adjacent. West is torn to pieces and borne into the vault, his head carried off by Clapham-Lee; when servants

4

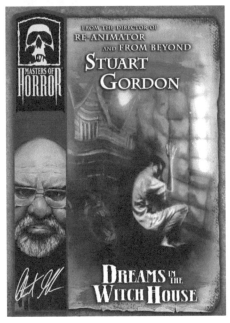

find the narrator unconscious in the morning, the wall is intact, and the police dismiss what little he says . . .

Scenarist Dennis Paoli worked on all of Gordon's formal HPL efforts, plus *Castle Freak*; *Re-Animator* marked the sole screenwriting credit, shared with them, for actor William J. Norris, who later appeared in Gordon's Poe adaptation *The Pit and the Pendulum* (1991). *Re-Animator* draws from various parts of the story, while *Bride of Re-Animator* (1990) is loosely based on the last two episodes. Neither Gordon nor Paoli was involved with the latter, for which producer Brian Yuzna — who returned along with actors Jeffrey Combs, Bruce Abbott, and David Gale — assumed the director's chair, as he would on *Beyond Re-Animator* (2003) as well, and was credited on the script with Rick Fry and Woody Keith.

Re-Animator's prologue, set in a modern-day Zurich university, graphically depicts the attempt by West (Combs) to revive his mentor, Dr. Hans Gruber (Al Berry), a literally eye-popping failure ("the dosage was too large"). Robert Dawson's title sequence is a nice montage of medical drawings, but the music by Richard Band — brother of Empire Pictures founder Charles — is a shameful rip-off of Bernard Herrmann's immortal score for *Psycho* (1960). In its early scenes, the film is relatively faithful to Lovecraft's basic set-up, with West and his soon-to-be assistant, here dubbed Dan Cain (Abbott), meeting and sharing an apartment as third-year students at Arkham's Miskatonic Medical School.

At first, HPL's Halsey seems to be bifurcated into his onscreen analog (Robert Sampson), whose first name was shorn of an "L," and brain researcher Dr. Carl Hill (Gale), who has scant patience with West's revolutionary ideas. West immediately antagonizes the latter with his accusations that Hill's theories are not only out of date, but also plagiarized from Gruber. Halsey also provides a love interest in the form of his daughter, Megan (Barbara Crampton), who is engaged to Dan; Gordon endeared himself to me with a scene of them making love beneath the poster for Jonathan Demme's concert movie *Stop Making Sense* (1984), which as the result of one viewing made Talking Heads my second-favorite band.

Megan's immediate aversion to West is hardly assuaged when she finds Dan's cat, Rufus, which ostensibly died by misadventure, inside West's fridge. He reanimates Rufus, with typically disastrous results, and Dan intervenes when he finds West being attacked by the feline revenant in his basement lab, but as he brings the mangled cat back to life again, to prove the efficacy of his reagent to Dan, Megan makes an ill-timed entrance. Her father, outraged, expels West, yet with equally poor timing seeks a confrontation with Dan in the morgue just as he and West are in mid-experiment; Halsey is killed by their subject, who is stopped too late with a bone saw through the chest, then reanimated and straitjacketed.

The film then begins to tack further from HPL and more toward black humor as Dr. Hill, having deduced that Halsey is actually dead, blackmails West to obtain his secret, only to be decapitated with a shovel and — as in the schlock classic *The Brain*

That Wouldn't Die (1962) — find his head in a pan. But West unwisely reanimates both body and head, with the former knocking him out before decamping with the latter and the reagent. Obsessed with Meg, Hill sends the lobotomized Halsey to kidnap her, and she awakens stark naked on a gurney with the head beside her; in the film's most notorious scene, the body holds it up as he licks her, but fortunately, the cavalry arrives just as it is placed between her legs.

West mocks Hill's academic aspirations — "Who's going to believe a talking head? Get a job in a sideshow" — as Dan frees Meg, but underestimates this "headless physician with the power of reanimating the dead." The morgue's inhabitants arise at the behest of Hill, whose laser-drill lobotomies effect mastery over them (it had been visually implied if not stated, let alone explained, that he also has hypnotic powers), and they attack West *et al.* Yet his mastery is less complete than he thinks, for Halsey retains sufficient autonomy to intercede on Meg's behalf, crushing Hill's head with his hands; the body, injected with a double-barreled overdose of the reagent by West, begins mutating wildly and seizes him.

As the zombie horde bursts from the morgue, West is last seen amid the chaos and smoke battling Hill's tentacular entrails and, begging Dan to save his work, tosses him a satchel containing the unbreakable plastic bottle of his reagent. Although Dan manages to sever its still-clutching arm with a fire axe, one of the revenants chokes Megan to death as they flee in the elevator, and the film ends with him in the E.R., having come full circle. As at the beginning, Dan is urged by Dr. Harrod (Carolyn Purdy-Gordon, the wife of Stuart) to give up when defibrillation fails to revive his flatlined patient; conventional means being ineffective, Dan injects the reagent into Meg, whose scream is heard over the fade-out . . .

Re-Animator was at first envisioned as a stage production for Gordon's Organic Theater Company, then as a half-hour television pilot, and then as a one-hour pilot, but was only considered bankable as a feature, which was picked up for distribution by Band's Empire Pictures. So extreme with its over-the-top gore and full-frontal nudity that it was released unrated, it was a hit in spite of the attendant commercial restrictions. An R-rated version, produced without his or Yuzna's involvement by Vestron Video, supplanted some of the more gruesome bits with scenes Gordon had cut for pacing before the picture's theatrical release (some of which augmented, albeit still without explaining, the hypnosis subplot).

Genre fans may recall Sampson as the father in Richard Matheson's classic *Twilight Zone* episode "Little Girl Lost" (3/16/62), while Peter Kent, playing his killer ("Melvin the Re-Animated"), became Arnold Schwarzenegger's longtime stunt double in *The Terminator* (1984), which according to Gordon's laserdisc audio commentary was filmed just prior to *Re-Animator* at L.A.'s S and A Studios.

Gordon, Yuzna, Paoli (all of whom shared credit for the adaptation, with a final screenplay by Paoli), Combs, and Crampton were reunited on *From Beyond*. First published in the pioneering fan magazine *The Fantasy Fan* (June 1934), Lovecraft's original short story was also reprinted in *Weird Tales* (February 1938).

Once again, the nameless narrator is the best friend of Crawford Tillinghast — a surname also used by HPL in **The Case of Charles Dexter Ward** (1927), adapted by legendary *TZ* scribe Charles Beaumont into Roger Corman's **The Haunted Palace** (1963). He'd been driven out of Tillinghast's attic laboratory, with its "accursed electrical machine," after learning "toward what goal his physical and metaphysical researches were leading," and responding with "awed and almost frightened remonstrances . . ." Ten weeks later, he is summoned back from his exile to "the ancient, lonely house set back from Benevolent Street" to find Tillinghast horribly changed: emaciated, discolored, twitching, unkempt.

Stating that "strange, inaccessible worlds exist at our very elbows," invisible to our "five feeble senses," Tillinghast can "generate waves acting on unrecognised sense-organs that exist in us as atrophied or rudimentary vestiges." Preparing to demonstrate his machine, which emits visible ultra-violet, he calls the pineal gland "the great sense-organ of organs [that] transmits visual pictures to the brain . . . the evidence from *beyond*." As the narrator begins receiving *outré* impressions, Tillinghast warns him to keep still: "in these rays *we are able to be seen as well as to see*," and when the housekeeper turned on the downstairs lights against orders, all of the servants had vanished, leaving "empty heaps of clothes . . . "

The narrator sees "[i]ndescribable shapes both alive and otherwise . . . mixed in disgusting array," most notably "great inky, jellyfish monstrosities" that devour one another while passing "through what we know as solids," even his own body. But Tillinghast has lured him there to exact revenge for his lack of encouragement, intending that he fall victim to "the ultimate beings I have discovered." The ending reveals that the narrator, armed with a revolver, had shot and shattered the machine; believing that he had been "hypnotised by the vindictive and homicidal madman," who is found dead of apoplexy, the police had released him,

but never found the bodies of the servants they say Tillinghast murdered.

The tree that grew from this tiny acorn repeats the dueling-scientists dynamic, although at first, Miskatonic's Dr. Crawford Tillinghast (Combs) is assisting S&M freak Dr. Edward Pretorious (Ted Sorel) with the Resonator, which stimulates the pineal gland and sunders interdimensional barriers. Crawford is blamed and presumed insane after a monster bites his mentor's head off, but over the objections of Dr. Bloch (Carolyn Purdy-Gordon), Dr. Katherine McMichaels (Crampton), a schizophrenia expert, brings him back to the lab to recreate the experiment, escorted by Sgt. Buford "Bubba" Brownlee (Ken Foree). When the machine is reactivated, she sees a deformed Pretorious and realizes Crawford is sane.

Influenced by the Resonator and compelled to activate it again, Katherine is menaced by Pretorious, and Crawford partly swallowed by a gigantic worm in the basement — leaving him bald — before it is shut down. She then tries to seduce Bubba, who is killed by bees when the Resonator turns itself back on, while Pretorious makes Crawford's pineal gland emerge from his forehead before Katherine disables

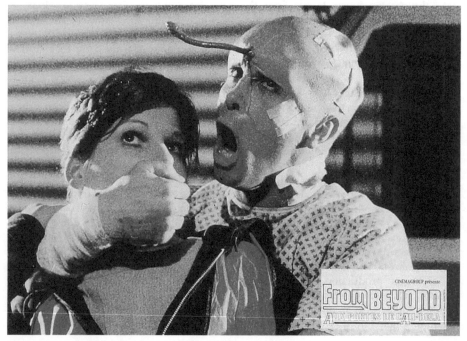

the machine with a fire extinguisher. She brings him back to the hospital, where the brain-hungry Crawford runs amok, killing Bloch and others; escaping amidst the confusion, Katherine returns to the lab with a time-bomb, planning to destroy the Resonator once and for all, and is followed by Crawford.

In the chaotic climax, Pretorious twists Crawford's head off and seizes Katherine, only to have Crawford emerge from his malleable body; the two crazed scientists tear each other to pieces, disintegrating into a disgusting mess as Katherine leaps out the window before the bomb explodes, leaving her hopelessly insane. Crampton's character is the antithesis of her earlier damsel in distress, sporting a black leather dominatrix outfit and craving the literally unearthly pleasures offered by the world beyond. Best known as Peter in George A. Romero's *Dawn of the Dead* (1978), Foree can be seen in Rob Zombie's *The Devil's Rejects* (2005), *Halloween* (2007), *Halloween II* (2009), and *The Lords of Salem* (2012).

Before formally returning to the HPL canon, Gordon was a writer on *Honey, I Shrunk the Kids* (1989), *Body Snatchers* (1993) — both of which he was originally set to direct — *The Dentist* (1996), and *Progeny* (1998). He was the director of *Dolls* (1987), the TV-movie *Daughter of Darkness* (1990), *Fortress* (1992), and Ray Bradbury's *The Wonderful Ice Cream Suit* (1998), which he'd directed on stage, and served in both capacities on *Robot Jox* (1989) and *Space Truckers* (1996). *Dagon* is based on the eponymous story but, like *The Haunted Palace*, also draws from HPL's **The Shadow over Innsmouth** (1936), which Paoli (who wrote the script), Yuzna, and Gordon long hoped to adapt under its own title.

A brief, early tale that debuted in *The Vagrant* (November 1919), and was later reprinted in *Weird Tales* (October 1923), "Dagon" is told by another nameless narrator, who can no longer afford the morphine that lets him forget, and plans to hurl himself from his garret window. Adrift in the Pacific, after escaping from a packet captured by the Germans in World War I,

he wakes to find himself "half sucked into a slimy expanse of hellish black mire." Crawling into his nearby boat, he theorizes that, due to a volcanic upheaval, "a portion of the ocean floor must have been thrown to the surface, exposing regions which for innumerable millions of years had lain hidden under unfathomable watery depths."

Once the soil has dried enough to explore, he ascends a large mound with a deep chasm beyond, a body of water at the bottom and a huge, white stone monolith on the opposite slope. Its surface bears both hieroglyphics of aquatic symbols and bas-relief carvings of oversized creatures, "damnably human in general outline despite webbed hands and feet, shockingly wide and flabby lips, glassy, bulging eyes, and other features less pleasant to recall." A "[v]ast, Polyphemus-like, and loathsome" monster surfaces and darts to the monolith, "about which it flung its gigantic scaly arms, the while it bowed its hideous head and gave vent to certain measured sounds. I think I went mad then," he recounts.

Only dimly recalling his frantic return to the boat and an ensuing storm, he came to his senses in a San Francisco hospital, having been picked up by an American ship, but his account is disbelieved, and a "celebrated ethnologist" is merely amused by his "peculiar questions regarding the ancient Philistine legend of Dagon, the Fish-God . . . " Since then he has dreamed of the day when "nameless things . . . may rise above the billows to drag down in their reeking talons the remnants of puny, war-exhausted mankind . . . " His hasty scrawling concludes: "The end is near. I hear a noise at the door, as of some immense slippery body lumbering against it. It shall not find me. God, *that hand!* The window!"

Innsmouth explains the federal government's "strange and secret investigation of certain conditions in the ancient Massachusetts seaport," involving the destruction of waterfront houses, mass arrests that left the town almost depopulated, and a "deep-diving submarine that discharged torpedoes downward in the marine abyss just beyond

Devil Reef." The narrator (again unnamed in the story, but identified in HPL's notes as Robert Olmstead) notes that in July 1927, "I was celebrating my coming of age by a tour of New England — sightseeing, antiquarian, and genealogical . . . " The cheapest route to Arkham, "whence my mother's family was derived," is a rickety bus that goes through shunned Innsmouth.

Staying over in Newburyport, he learns of the 1846 epidemic that reduced Innsmouth's population to about 400, and the Marsh refinery whose gold ingots — source unknown — are now the sole industry. Its founder, Captain Obed Marsh, is said to have found a pirate cache on Devil Reef, perhaps accounting for the strange local jewelry, exemplified by an unearthly tiara. The popularity of a secret cult, the Esoteric Order of Dagon, coincided with a resurgence in abundant fishing, while some of the townsfolk "have queer narrow heads with flat noses and bulgy, stary eyes that never seem to shut, and their skin ain't quite right. Rough and scabby . . . the sides of their necks are all shriveled or creased up."

Intrigued, Robert boards Innsmouth man Joe Sargent's bus the next morning, passing the former Masonic Hall now housing the cult, and a nearby church whose robed pastor bears a tiara matching the one displayed at the Newburyport Historical Society. He checks his valise at the Gilman House, a shabby hotel where unnatural voices are heard at night, and learns that his best informant, if properly lubricated, will be the town drunkard, 96-year-old Zadok Allen; Barnabas Marsh, Obed's grandson, is never seen due to his deformities. Robert tours the town — with its furtive, shambling figures, rotting houses, and oppressive fishy smell — and plans to take the 8:00 bus for Arkham . . . until he catches sight of Zadok.

A quart of bootleg whiskey lures Zadok to an abandoned wharf, hidden from the hostile locals, where he tells of Obed trading for the jewelry with South Sea islanders who made twice-yearly human sacrifices to frog-like amphibians. Interbreeding resulted in human-looking children who gradually came to resemble them and eventually joined them in the sea, where they would live forever. The natives gave Obed a "lead thingumajig" to bring up the "fish-things"; after finding them wiped out by other islanders, protected by charms like those used by "the lost Old Ones," he set up shop on Devil Reef, and when his arrest by concerned citizens halted the offerings, the "epidemic" — a piscine massacre — ensued.

After making dire hints about the creatures' future plans ("ever hear tell of a *shoggoth*?"), Zadok warns, "*They seen us* — git aout fer your life!," and flees in terror, never to be seen again. Engine trouble forces Robert to stay at the Gilman, where the bolted doors of his fourth-story room are furtively tried, and absent a fire escape, he breaks into connecting rooms to escape via a neighboring rooftop. Shambling pursuers pour out of the Gilman, cutting off all roads leading from town, so he follows an abandoned railway, fainting as he sees from concealment "the blasphemous fish-frogs . . . in which there was no mixture of the normal at all . . . .in a limitless stream — flopping, hopping, croaking, bleating . . . "

The next day Robert reaches Arkham, where long talks with government officials set in motion the eventual raids, and he learns from the curator of the historical society that his great-grandfather, Benjamin Orne (another surname in **Charles Dexter Ward**), married a Marsh. Discovering that she owned some of the golden jewelry, he realizes that she was Obed's daughter, and muses, "Who — or *what* — then, was my great-great-grandmother?" She is Pth'thya-l'yi, whom he meets in a dream, and who after Obed's death returned to Y'ha-nthlei, the city of the Deep Ones; they plan to unleash amorphous *shoggoths* upon humanity to exact "the tribute Great Cthulhu craved," and he eagerly awaits joining them.

Dagon opens as dotcom genius Paul Marsh (Ezra Godden) has a recurring dream about a deadly mermaid aboard a boat off the coast of Spain (where the film was shot) owned by his investor, the archly named Howard (Brendan Price). A squall thrusts it into rocks that breach the hull and pinion Howard's wife, Vicki

(Birgit Bofarull), so Paul — who sports a Miskatonic sweatshirt — and his girlfriend, Barbara (Raquel Meroño), take the raft to seek help in a nearby village, Imboca, a rough Spanish translation of Innsmouth. They find a Priest (Ferran Lahoz), who has webbed hands and recruits some Imbocans to help, taking Paul to the boat, but he insists that Barbara must remain behind to speak with the police.

En route to the hotel in search of a phone, she is unnerved by examples of "the Innsmouth look," as HPL called it, and once there, she is seized by the Priest and a mute receptionist (José Lifante). Reaching the boat, Paul finds no trace of the couple, nor a sign of Barbara at the hotel, so he takes a decrepit room, from which he sees a sinister crowd in the street below coming after him, and escapes as in the story. Paul falls into a warehouse where he finds Howard's skin hanging, and after eluding the mob he encounters Zadok's cinematic equivalent, Ezequiel, played by Francisco Rabal, who had appeared in William Friedkin's *Sorcerer* (1977), and died shortly before *Dagon*'s release (the film was dedicated to him).

Ezequiel tells Paul that Barbara and Vicki are dead and, via flashbacks, relates a potted version of HPL's backstory, with Orpheus Cambarro (Alfredo Villa) as the Obed analog, whose sacrilege extends to killing a Catholic priest (Fernando Gil) with a sledgehammer. Young Ezequiel (Victor Barreira) watched in horror as his father (Javier Sandoval) had his throat cut and his mother (Uxía Blanco) was carried off. The only car in Imboca is owned by Orpheus's grandson, Xavier (Juan Minguell), so Paul tries to hot-wire it while Ezequiel — tolerated because he is thought crazy — distracts Xavier's minions, but Paul accidentally sounds the horn and, in desperation, he breaks into the Cambarro mansion.

There, Paul stumbles into the bedroom of Xavier's daughter, Uxía (Macarena Gómez), the image of the mermaid, who says she has been waiting for him, although her attempted seduction fails when he pulls back the covers to reveal her gills and tentacles. He flees and — after bludgeoning

the chauffeur (Diego Herberg) with his cell phone — grabs the keys for a getaway, yet crashes the car during a rain-swept skirmish with the Imbocans, who knock him out after he is forced to defend himself from a horrific hybrid. He wakes to find he is imprisoned with Ezequiel, Barbara, and Vicki, who are not dead, but Vicki has lost a leg in the accident, and swears that a monster has planted something inside her.

During a failed breakout, Vicki grabs a knife and kills herself, and Barbara is taken away from Paul, who is forced to watch while the Priest flays Ezequiel alive, chanting "*Iä! Iä! Cthulhu fhtagn!*" Saved from the same fate by Uxía, who claims him as her own and has him freed, Paul kills the Priest and his tanners (Igancio Carreño, Joan Manel Vadel) with their own implements, then locates Dagon's underground temple, where the Imbocans — like Leatherface — wear their victims' skins, and Priestess Uxía is having a naked Barbara lowered into a stone well. Paul sets the worshippers aflame with cans of kerosene, but is too late to save Barbara as Dagon drags her down, leaving her manacled arms dangling . . .

Beaten down by the remaining mob, Paul is shown to be developing gills and learns from Uxía that his mother was married to Xavier, who brought outsiders to Imboca; while Paul and Uxía had different mothers, both are children of Dagon. Refusing her desire to give brotherly love a whole new meaning, he douses and ignites himself, but she hurls herself into his flaming form, carrying them both into the well, and as they descend, Paul seems resigned to his fate. **Innsmouth**'s last line ("We shall . . . dive down through black abysses to Cyclopean and many-columned Y'ha-nthlei, and in that lair of the Deep Ones we shall dwell amidst wonder and glory forever") is paraphrased to serve as the closing epigram.

Previously adapted, uncredited, as Vernon Sewell's *Curse of the Crimson Altar* (aka *The Crimson Cult*, 1968), HPL's "The Dreams in the Witch-House" (*Weird Tales*, July 1933) is also set in Arkham. In the unpopular manse, Miskatonic student Walter Gilman rents the attic room once occupied by Keziah Mason, who in 1692 vanished from Salem Gaol while "a small, white-fanged furry thing" scuttled out of her cell. Seeking "to connect his mathematics with the fantastic legends of elder magic," he correlates inklings from the **Necronomicon** and similar "dubious old books on forbidden secrets . . . with his abstract formulae on the properties of space and the linkage of dimensions known and unknown."

Obsessed with the room's "peculiar angles" — its slanting wall and ceiling betray a long-sealed loft above — Gilman dreams of an aged Mason, who says "He must meet the Black Man [Nyarlathotep], and . . . sign in his own blood the book of Azathoth," and her murine familiar, Brown Jenkin, with its oddly human face and paws. He is also transported into fantastic, other-dimensional realms, but after apparently participating in the sacrifice of a missing child while sleep-walking, Gilman is killed as Brown Jenkin tunnels through his body and eats his heart. Found amid the debris when the roof collapses years later are fragments of mystical books and papers, plus "a veritable ossuary" of children's bones.

In Showtime's version, also starring Godden, Keziah (Susanna Uchatius) beds Walter in a naked, nubile form before reverting to a crone, and his fellow student lodger is now a single mother, Frances Elwood (Chelah Horsdal), which personalizes the victim, her baby Danny (David and Nicholas Racz). But Gordon and Paoli's modernization is generally faithful, with Brown Jenkin (Yevgen Voronin) in makeup effects from Gregory Nicotero and Howard Berger. Gordon also directed Mamet's own adaptation of his play *Edmond* that same year, and later returned to Poe with "The Black Cat" (1/19/07), another *Masters of Horror* episode co-written with Paoli; he died (of multiple organ failure) at 72 in 2020.

Texts cited:
The Complete Fiction of H.P. Lovecraft (Norwalk, CT: Easton Press, 2017).

• • •

Caroline Munro
FIRST LADY OF FANTASY

The Spy Who Loved Me Contact Sheet

ONCE UPON A TIME... AT THE NEW BEVERLY

A night with Quentin Tarantino celebrating the release of his first novel

by Duane Swierczynski

Cliff drives past Pink's Hot Dogs, on the corner of La Brea and Melrose. There are so many people outside crowded around the hot-dog stand, you'd think they were giving away free pussy, not selling overpriced chili dogs. Cliff moves the Cadillac into the right-hand lane and makes a right when he gets to Beverly Boulevard. He drives a short distance down Beverly and pulls up in front of a little movie theater and parks the car.

— **Once Upon a Time in Hollywood**
by Quentin Tarantino

I've made this same drive many times since moving to Los Angeles, though with a few differences. I never thought Pink's dogs were overpriced. (If they're tasty enough to drag Harlan Ellison out of his house at midnight, as depicted in his short story "Prince Myshkin, and Hold the Relish," they can charge whatever they like.) But more importantly: I never turn right at Beverly. I turn right a block north, at Oakwood, because that's where you can find the best parking. Only in the movies can you pull up and find a free space directly in front of the theater, no parking meters, no time limits.

I made this same drive on June 29, 2021, the night the New Beverly Cinema hosted a book launch party for writer, director (and theater owner) Quentin Tarantino. I've been eager to read his **Once Upon a Time in Hollywood** (note the lack of ellipses, unlike the film) novelization since I first heard about it. The chance to be there, on pub day, with Tarantino himself? Yes, please.

For a moment, this was the hottest ticket in town. Most of us knew the day tickets would go on sale, but we didn't know the exact time. I kept checking the site, and thought I was in luck when I refreshed the site just all of the tickets for that month were released. But seconds later . . . *sold out*. Which was not surprising; New Bev fans are like rabid attack dogs. Tickets to their annual All-Night Horror Show are always gone in 60 seconds, if not sooner. You need a trigger finger like a gunslinger on that refresh button.

Something told me to try again a few minutes later, just in case there was a glitch. And maybe there was, because . . . lo! . . . I was miraculously able to score a seat — and in my favorite section of the theater, too (the section on the right, four seats wide, cocked at the perfect angle to enjoy the show even if Manute Bol sits in front of you). Sometimes, the Cinema Gods take pity on their worshippers.

There were metal detectors in front of the theater; this was a new thing. There was also a strict no cell phone policy, which meant I couldn't take my usual marquee photo before every New Bev show.

Then again, this was no typical New Bev show. This may have been my first time to the theater for something other than watching a movie.

I'm not a religious man, but since I moved to L.A. in 2016 the New Bev has become my church. The aroma of the popcorn is like incense to me, transporting me to a higher cinematic plane where they show movies on 35mm film, and often two at a time — if not more. I've dragged plenty of friends along with me to worship, but I'm just as happy to go alone. Laughing and gasping with strangers is just as satisfying as speaking in tongues.

When the New Beverly temporarily closed in 2018 for renovations, it was a serious blow. Covid-19 closed it again in March 2020, right in the middle of an amazing run of movies (including *Squirm* and *Tender Flesh*, which I saw there on the 3rd). When I felt safe enough to return to movie theaters, I broke my fast with two Brucesploitation flicks: *Kung Fu's Hero* and *The Young Dragon*. I was ready to believe again. Scoring a ticket to Tarantino's book launch party pretty much brought me to my knees in gratitude.

But first, it brought me a gift bag. Each attendee received a copy of the paperback, along with bookmarks, buttons and a rubbery, 1970s-style New Bev keychain. The New Bev likes to spoil its audience. On my bookshelf is a *Suspiria* mug I received after attending a Dario Argento all-nighter; I adore my New Bev vampire cap (scored after a night of horror comedies back in 2016). If I ever sent you a book in the mail, it usually comes with a short note on the back of a New Bev postcard, supplied to patrons free of charge. You can keep your fancy-pants Chateau Marmont stationery; all of the really cool elevator pitches are scribbled on the back of New Bev postcards.

I sat in my chair and tried to continue reading the paperback, but I needed more light, and since my phone was in my glove box, I simply sat there in worshipful silence. Okay, not exactly. The theater was playing vintage highlights from KHJ Los Angeles radio. I also scanned the crowd to see if maybe Cliff or Rick was among the masked humans in the audience.

And then Quentin arrived, and everyone in the theater lost their minds.

The good news is that you can experience this part of the book launch for yourself. The Reel Cinema podcast episode (July 6, 2021) is deep dive and a sheer delight.

Now here are the parts you missed.

Tarantino read a few short selections from the novel. For the first, he asked the audience to imagine Samuel L. Jackson as the speaker—a French pimp who Cliff Booth encounters when he's slumming around Europe after WWII. Usually, I'm not a fan of authors reading their own work. Very few do it well. Tarantino — along with James Ellroy — are the rare exceptions. This is because they know a reading is not about the words on the page but the performance, and Tarantino performed like a stone-cold motherfucker. I haven't laughed that hard at the New Beverly since watching *Pieces*.

(Later, I read the same sequence in the book, while it was still gloriously ribald and hilarious — it was missing that extra *something*. In this case, Tarantino-as-Samuel-L-Jackson saying things like, "There ain't no fuck-free holiday for a true *maq*.")

Next, Tarantino read from a scene where Cliff Booth is explaining to Rick Dalton what it's like to kill a man. I found myself dearly wishing this had been included in the film, and not just because it's a wonderfully dark and weird moment. No — this is because this scene takes place at the Smoke House, which is Burbank's answer to Hollywood's Musso & Frank Grill, and one of my favorite L.A. haunts. George Clooney loved the place so much he named his production company after it. Friends have treated me there; I've treated friends there. However, none of my friends have ever offered to buy me a live pig so that I could stab it repeatedly then hold on to the poor suffering animal as its life drained from its body. Then again, who among us has friends like Cliff Booth?

A word about Mr. Booth, who is easily my favorite character in the movie. Cliff is the kind of guy Charles Willeford called a "blithe psychopath" — you may disapprove of what he does ("I don't dig him," in the words of Kurt Russell's Randy Miller), but you can't help rooting for the guy anyway.

So, I was very happy to learn there

was a whole lotta Cliff Booth in the novel — including a definitive answer to the question that nagged most of us for almost two years: *Did he, or didn't he?* But the Cliff Booth you meet on the page is not quite the Cliff on screen. No spoilers here, but there's a lot more "psychopath" to the character without the easygoing charm of Brad Pitt.

The night ended with Tarantino signing copies of the paperback for everyone in the theater, which was a real treat. I struck up a conversation with the masked dude sitting next to me, only to learn it was fellow crime writer J. David Gonzalez. It's easy to talk movies with a fellow New Bev-goer; it's something else to meet someone who can do a deep dive into, say, Florida crime novelists. Time flew by talking to David, and when the New Bev's Phil Blankenship approached to say hello, he assumed David and I were old war buddies.

Finally, I approached Tarantino at his table. He was in high spirits, and charming as fuck. Technically, I've met him before. During the New Bev premiere of Sophia Coppola's *The Beguiled*, I spied him sitting a few rows back, so I worked up the courage to walk up and thank him for keeping the New Bev alive. He was gracious, but probably a little befuddled by this random dude who didn't even have an interesting movie question to ask.

This time, however, I was prepared. I had a question in my back pocket that I'd been dying to ask since seeing *OUATIH* (at the New Bev, of course).

"Did you personally choose the paperback books in Cliff Booth's trailer?" I asked.

This was a legit obsession of mine. When *OUITAH* was finally available on home video, I froze that scene and tried to read the spines.

And the answer?

"Of course!" Tarantino bellowed.

Now in a perfect world I would have followed up with questions about Cliff's taste in mid-century paperback fiction. I was convinced Cliff would have been a Gold Medal reader, and quite likely a Donald Hamilton man. But instead, I followed up with . . .

"Oh, and my first name is D-U-A-N-E . . . the only way to spell it!"

"The only way!" Tarantino agreed.

(I admit, this was not a conversation that would go down in literary history.)

Tarantino signed many books to so-and-so "with love" that night. QT's penmanship is notoriously "loose"; my friend (and fellow *bare•bones* contributor) David J. Schow vowed to refer to me as "Ovane Wilove" from now on. But screw Schow. That signed copy will live on my bookshelf with my other favorite novelizations: Alan Dean Foster's *Dark Star*, Alan Sharp's *Night Moves*, Paddy Chayefsky's *Altered States*.

Calling this paperback a novelization, however, is not quite accurate — it's more of a prose version of Blu Ray extras, with deep character dives and back stories to things only hinted at on screen. I adored the book, but also pity the person who approaches it cold without having watched the movie. For one thing, the entire third act is covered in an off-handed remark. For another, there are lengthy diversions not only into cinematic history, but also the full plot of the movie's fictional western, *Lancer*. At times, you wonder if you're reading a novel or some other literary form that lives in the haze between a movie tie-in, memoir, background notes, and some Hollywood bullshit a quivering drunk is telling you in some dive at 1 AM.

Which reminds me of the most striking thing about the book party. At times (and you can hear this on the podcast), Tarantino lapsed into talking about his fictional characters as if they're real people, interacting with celebrities from our universe. Celebrities like Aldo Ray and Hayley Mills and . . . well, Quentin Tarantino, who makes a cameo appearance in the novel. (Minor spoiler: he's only six years old.) After a while, the border between our world and Tarantino's world begins to blur. And that's the best way to describe the appeal of *any* night at the New Bev, with 21st Century distractions (climate change, plagues, attempted coups) kept outside with the cell phones. I happen to enjoy that world. I visit as often as I can.

• • •

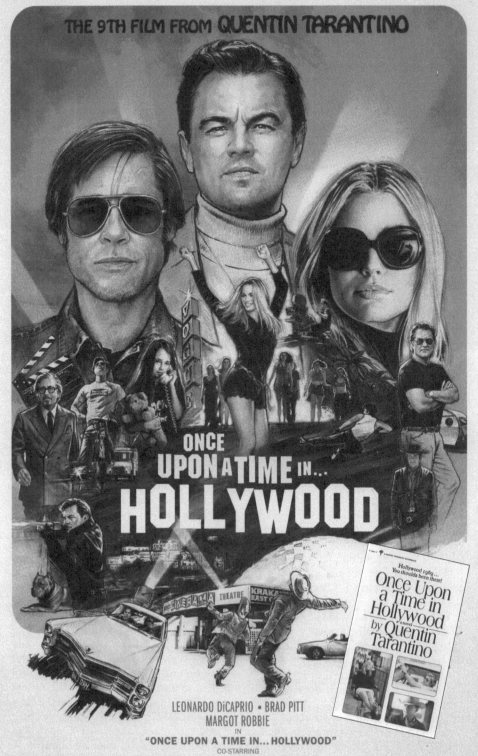

THE 9TH FILM FROM QUENTIN TARANTINO

ONCE
UPON A TIME in...
HOLLYWOOD

Hollywood 1969...
You shoulda been there!

ONCE
Upon
a Time in
Hollywood
by
Quentin
Tarantino

a novel

LEONARDO DiCAPRIO • BRAD PITT
MARGOT ROBBIE
IN
"ONCE UPON A TIME IN... HOLLYWOOD"
CO-STARRING
EMILE HIRSCH • MARGARET QUALLEY • TIMOTHY OLYPHANT • AUSTIN BUTLER • DAKOTA FANNING • BRUCE DERN and AL PACINO
COLUMBIA PICTURES Presents • In Association with BONA FILM GROUP CO., LTD. • A HEYDAY FILMS Production • A Film by QUENTIN TARANTINO
Casting By VICTORIA THOMAS, CSA • Costume Designer ARIANNE PHILLIPS • Film Editor FRED RASKIN, ACE • Production Designer BARBARA LING
Director of Photography ROBERT RICHARDSON, ASC • Executive Producers GEORGIA KACANDES • YU DONG • JEFFREY CHAN
Produced by DAVID HEYMAN • SHANNON McINTOSH • QUENTIN TARANTINO • Written and Directed by QUENTIN TARANTINO

Read the Harper Perennial Paperback   IN THEATERS JULY 26   #OnceUponATimeInHollywood   SONY
OnceUponATimeInHollywood.Movie

bare•bones ZOOMS IN ON
Quentin Tarantino's **Once Upon a Time in Hollywood**
A roundtable discussion on the novelization of his film

Nearly 20 years ago, Miramax Books (formerly Talk Miramax Books) acquired the rights to publish Quentin Tarantino's **Kill Bill: A Novel**.

In an article on thebookseller.com in 2002, Rod Stewart (no, not that one) noted, "Talk has retained a sharp reputation, signing film director Quentin Tarantino's novel **Kill Bill** *for publication six months before the cinema release of his film adaptation next November. Rights have been sold to publishers in 16 territories, including Fourth Estate in the UK."*

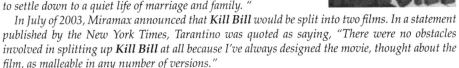

Ultimately scheduled for publication on August 1st, 2003, the title was solicited on Amazon with a cover thumbnail and the following description:

*"***Kill Bill** *is Tarantino's debut novel, an extraordinary work of fiction that will speak powerfully to his many admirers. It's the story of The Bride, a world-class assassin and a retired member of the elite, all-female Deadly Viper Assassination Squad (DiVAS), who's ready to settle down to a quiet life of marriage and family. "*

In July of 2003, Miramax announced that **Kill Bill** *would be split into two films. In a statement published by the New York Times, Tarantino was quoted as saying, "There were no obstacles involved in splitting up* **Kill Bill** *at all because I've always designed the movie, thought about the film, as malleable in any number of versions."*

While it's understandable that the splitting of the film into two parts might delay the novel's release, I was disappointed that even following the release of **Kill Bill: Volume 2** *in 2004, there was no further word on the novel. Whether the book was never completed or pulled from publication for some other reason remains a mystery.*

Flash forward 17 years. In the summer of 2021, we were finally treated to Quentin Tarantino's first prose fiction: a self-proclaimed novelization of his ninth film, **Once Upon a Time... in Hollywood**. *To celebrate this historic event, I was honored to assemble an amazing group of writers in a Zoom session to discuss Quentin's first novel. I was joined by Stephen R. Bissette, Kim Newman, David J. Schow and Duane Swierczynski. We talked for several hours — a transcript of which follows.*

Be aware that we do dive deeply into spoiler territory, so keep that in mind if you haven't yet seen the film or read the book. I hope you enjoy the discussion as much as we did.

— John Scoleri

John: Before we talk about the novelization, I want to start by asking everyone to share their thoughts on the film, to establish where we were each coming from when we picked up the book.

Stephen: Well, hell. Me first, then? OK — I loved it. Stem to stern, love at first sight. I caught it at a local theater, first matinee show. I loved the whole experience, but I wasn't in any way prepared for where it took me, where it left me: I'd never felt anything like the final minutes of the movie made me feel, not in any movie, not at any time in my entire life — so, yes, I loved it, I love it still.

At the time, I urged folks to avoid reading anything about the movie, to just go and see *Once Upon a Time... in Hollywood*, and that if you do see it, don't pick up to leave until the full credits run their course (there's a visual treat mid-way through the credits, and an audio treat closes out the credits). I also prepared kind of a 'cue sheet' to let younger potential viewers know all they'd need to know going in; posted it on social media, had a little printout copy for friends and students who'd expressed interest in seeing it.*

I thought the film sported a fantastic ensemble cast who gave their all throughout, led by Leonardo DiCaprio & Brad Pitt — they're the heart of the film and narrative, but the rich tapestry is fueled by an unfolding cast of characters and characterizations from Margot Robbie (radiant as Tate), Emile Hirsch, Margaret Qualley, Timothy Olyphant, Austin Butler, Dakota Fanning, Bruce Dern, Al Pacino, Zoë Bell, Kurt Russell, and Luke Perry (in his final big-screen role), among others. I was a teenager when the events the film springboarded from actually took place, though I've only visited Los Angeles and California as an adult; to my eyes and

mind, the movie evoked a great sense of the time and place and era (1969, and previous years). I found it only occasionally compromised in very minor ways, by my eye/recall. All in all, it's definitely one of Tarantino's finest, up there with *Jackie Brown*, taken on its own leisurely terms. Deft, playful, engaging storytelling throughout, an impeccably mounted production and execution, great slow-burn suspense in a couple key passages (which reminded me in their way of some of the most potent passages in David Fincher's 2007 *Zodiac*,), and if you love westerns and Italian films the way I love 'em, you'll find much to enjoy. The three-act structure is flawless, and brilliantly conceived and executed.

My second experience of the film, in a theater, turned out to be an ideal unplanned double-bill one summer day, when I caught *Echo in the Canyon* (a documentary about the Laurel Canyon/L.A. 1960s music scene) and revisited *Once Upon a Time... in Hollywood* the same afternoon. This made for absolute cinematic bliss — the only way it could have been better is if I'd somehow crammed in screening either *Model Shop* (1968) or *Beyond the Valley of the Dolls* (1970) the same day.

On second viewing, given the controversy immediately kicking up on social media about the Bruce Lee sequence, Tarantino's Bruce Lee appears in three scenes: Cliff's flashback (the fight with Cliff), another flashback with Sharon, and a 'real time' shot in the August sequence of Jay Sebring (Emile Hirsch) training outside of the Tate house with Lee. The latter two scenes present Lee in a very favorable, even sweet, light; honestly, while I understand Bruce Lee's daughter taking umbrage, I don't think anyone else has anything to complain about. I appreciate the context and revisions the parallel

* Here's what I offered: "All you need to know going in (no spoilers): yep, there were TV westerns on every network every day of the week in the late 1950s and early 1960s; Sharon Tate's breakthrough roles in *Eye of the Devil* (1966) and especially *Valley of the Dolls* (1967) were followed by prominent roles in Roman Polanski's *The Fearless Vampire Killers* (*Dance of the Vampires*, 1967) and the lame but very popular Dean Martin/Matt Helm opus *The Wrecking Crew* (1969); she was also prominently featured in billboard and print ads for Coppertone; Bruce Lee played Kato on the William (*Batman*) Dozier-produced TV series *The Green Hornet*; after it ceased to be a popular set for TV and movie western filming, Charles Manson and his cult followers took over the essentially abandoned Spahn Ranch; Polanski and Tate were wed on January 20, 1968, and moved in to 10050 Cielo Drive in Benedict Canyon (the previous home of Terry Melcher and Candice Bergen) on February 15, 1969; while Polanksi was in the UK working on his next project (an adaptation of the bestseller *Day of the Dolphin*), Charles Manson followers Tex Watson, Susan Atkins, Linda Kasabian, and Patricia Krenwinkel butchered Tate, her unborn child (8 months), Jay Sebring, Wojciech Frykowski, Abigail Folger, and Steven Parent in and just outside the Polanski/Tate home on August 9, 1969 (FYI, Leno and Rosemary LaBianca were murdered by Manson followers in their home the next day). Avoid reading anything else. If you know the above, it's all you need to know going in." — SRB

18

chapter in Quentin's novel bring to this central flashback, but it's a bit like Senator Mitch McConnell double-down on some completely bizarre ideological position he's taken: I, for one, didn't need any "justification." It's a fiction, constructed in part around real-life individuals presented as characters (Michelle Phillips, Steve McQueen, Roman Polanski, etc.); if anybody skipped or is skipping the movie out of some kind of twisted devotion to Bruce Lee, well, you'd better either never screen *Kentucky Fried Movie* and/or the umpteen faux-Bruce Lee movies of the 1970s, or sandblast your memory of having seen them. I can't see how *Once Upon a Time...* either tarnishes or taints Lee's memory, or the man.

While nothing will ever touch the first-time (unspoiled by expectations or any hint of what was coming) experience of seeing *Once Upon a Time... in Hollywood*, I have to say the film was even better the second time around, and rewards upon every screening since (via Blu-ray). While I doubt I could sway anyone in a debate on such matters, I have to say this remains one of the best films I caught in 2019, and is now a real favorite; I think it is perhaps Tarantino's best feature.

Kim: Quentin Tarantino's abiding passion – and major subject matter – has been the movies he grew up watching, augmented by TV and music of the same era, scrambled into a switching-channels-at-random pop culture melange which functions as a guide to the inside of his head but also to a dream of America that's distinct from the American dream. Here, with a title that evokes Sergio Leone, he conjures up the media landscape of Los Angeles in 1969, to the extent of filling the frame (and soundtrack) the way artist Jack Davis did (whose style is pastiched on mock posters and a *MAD Magazine* cover) to create a montage of that year . . . with celebs of the period played by contemporary faces that sort of match (Mike Moh as Bruce Lee, Damian Lewis as Steve McQueen, Rumer Willis as Joanna Pettet, Rachel Redleaf as Mama Cass), posters and marquees for real movies and invented ones slotted into

real filmographies, TV show excerpts, cars, radio ads, product packaging, fashions (lots of shots of boots), attitudes, hairstyles and trivia.

Fifty years is long enough for a year to be mythologized and misremembered in the creation of a genre – as proved by the Western. So, just as *Inglourious Basterds* was about the imagined WWII, not the real one – this is as much a wishful thinking version of the year of the Manson Murders and the Moon Landing as a recreation.

Manson slinks on in one scene – and, yet again, someone must be getting royalties for the use of a Manson-penned song on the soundtrack – that happens to overlap with the clutch of recent films on the subject (*Charlie Says, The Haunting of Sharon Tate, Wolves at the Door*). It's a long, episodic, discursive film – like previous *Once Upon a Time in . . .* movies – and has its own eight-month ellipsis in the middle as an agent persuades Rick to go to Italy and star in the kind of films Tarantino especially loves.

There's a fantastical thread to build up Cliff's near-superhuman skills – in a scene that proved to be controversial, he takes on Bruce Lee and does not get his Caucasian ass handed to him – and set up a climax (like *El Cid*) that rides off the pages of history and into the books of legend. Tarantino's love of stuff is infectious, and only he could stage a whole scene in which Margot Robbie goes to a movie-house and cheerfully watches the real Sharon Tate in *The Wrecking Crew* with childish pleasure. That Tarantino wants to associate this point in Hollywood history with Dean Martin as Matt Helm rather than, say, Paul Newman as Butch Cassidy or Dennis Hopper on a motorcycle is a hip-to-be-square moment and, though Rick growing his hair and Cliff smoking an acid-laced cigarette are key elements, this takes a stand for Marlboro Man values against anything vaguely hippie.

It's a rare Tarantino film without a significant African-American presence – Bruce Lee, quoting an actual interview, refers to Muhammad Ali as Cassius Clay – and it depicts the Manson clan as creepy spectres without referencing Manson's intent to foment a race war. Even the inspired music choices are whitebread. It's as interesting for what it leaves out as what it includes, but it's always interesting.

David: I'm gonna come at this completely backward, because I was not a fan of the movie when I saw it. And I hope Quentin will forgive me, because he's recently said some very kind things about me in interviews and podcasts. Oh, who am I kidding? Quentin would say, "I don't care what you think!"

If the movie had been done 20 years ago, then all that travelogue, all that shoe leather, might have been more interesting to me. Today, my eye says most viewers will just dismiss the detail as some kind of CGI trick, if they notice it at all. I need to explain "shoe leather," perhaps. It used to be a cheap way to use up running time when you were short on budget and resources, but you had to hit the 80- or 90-minute mark for a feature, whatever the minimum limit was. So if a character gets in a car, you show a long short of the car driving toward camera, then follow the car through a pass or a turn into a reverse angle where you spend just as much time showing the car driving away, getting smaller. There — you just used up 30 or 45 seconds that didn't impact the narrative at all when you could have just cut to the car arriving at whatever destination to get on with the next plot point. Same with people walking from one place to another, hence "shoe leather."

There's a lot of shoe leather in *Once Upon a Time... in Hollywood*. But I come away happy because it brought me to the

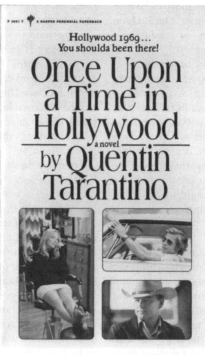

Hollywood 1969...
You shoulda been there!

Once Upon a Time in Hollywood
a novel
by Quentin Tarantino

book, which I didn't expect to like. Because the book is illuminating in the best way. I'll give you a major example and a minor example.

Major example: Bruce Lee. Lots of people interpreted the Bruce Lee scene as Quentin just being a dick to Bruce Lee. But in the book, that scene is completely contextualized.

Minor example: The dog. Now, unless you completely buy America's demonization of the pit bull (where the breed in fact was once "America's dog"), it helps to know that Brandy was *completely trained* to take down attackers in a scenario like that at the climax, partially because she was technically abused by Cliff as well — he trained her by dog-fighting her so she wouldn't get slaughtered.

So, except for the ending which kind of goes full-comedy (in the film), I found I generally liked each and every scene better in the book, for reasons I hope we'll get into.

John: I became a Quentin Tarantino fan after watching *Reservoir Dogs* on VHS. As a result of that, I was in the theater on opening night for *Pulp Fiction*, and was blown away. He once again exceeded my expectations with *Jackie Brown*, which soon became my favorite of his movies. And as much as I enjoyed his subsequent films, I honestly didn't expect that he would be able to top *Jackie Brown*. And then came *Once Upon a Time... in Hollywood*. I was lucky enough to catch a preview screening a few days before it opened, so I was able to avoid any spoilers beyond what I had seen in the trailers. Like most people who were aware of the film, I went in thinking I was going to see a film that would culminate in the Manson Family murders. So as I watched, I got to know Quentin's characters, as well as Sharon Tate — who, having grown up in the '70s, I really only ever knew of as a tabloid headline. As the events of the film unfolded, there was a lingering sense of dread because I knew — or thought I knew — the impending doom on the horizon. When Rick confronts Tex and the girls outside his house, I thought, Quentin is brilliant; he's going to save Sharon by sacrificing the characters we spent the last few hours getting to know and love. Boy, was I wrong about that. The climax of the film proved to be an uproarious, cathartic experience. I relished seeing the perpetrators of those horrible murders 50 years ago get their just desserts. And when finally given a chance to stop and take a breath, I was overcome by emotion because in this world — this fairy-tale world that Quentin had created — Sharon and her friends survived. It was an extremely powerful and unique first viewing experience. That said, I found myself compelled to see it again and again. All tolled, I saw it 10 times in the theater. While I still might pick Robert Forster's Max Cherry as my favorite performance in a Tarantino film, *Hollywood* is without a doubt my favorite of his films.

Duane: In some ways, I was scientifically pre-conditioned to love *Once Upon a Time... in Hollywood*. Ever since moving to L.A. five years ago, I've made the New Beverly my second home. And looking back, I realize that I was watching all kinds of films that served as Tarantino's inspirations for the movie. Manson-sploitation flicks.

Roman Polanski and Sharon Tate movies, specifically, *The Fearless Vampire Killers*. But most importantly, Westerns. So many Westerns. As an East Coast city kid, I never really paid much attention to the genre, but the New Bev made me fall in love with them, from *Navajo Joe* to *Ulzana's Raid*. So by the time I was sitting down to enjoy a Friday morning screening of *Hollywood*, I'd already been through a kind of Tarantino film school, preparing me for the fairy tale I was about to watch.

John: As we kick off our discussion of the novel, I'm interested in a couple of things. First, what were your expectations for the book, and also, what did you think of the look of the physical book. A lot of reviewers have said it looks just like a novelization from the period. Personally, I didn't feel that way when I first saw it.

Stephen: To me it looks like a 1980s novelization, like **Ragtime**.

Kim holds up a novelization of **A Bullet for Pretty Boy** *with a similar montage photo cover.*

Stephen: Oh there we go, **A Bullet for Pretty Boy**. Oh my God! Kim has the Larry Buchanan novelization, **A Bullet for Pretty Boy**! My fucking mind has been blown!

John holds up the back cover to the novelization of **Taxi Driver**, *which has a very similar photo montage to the* **Hollywood** *cover.*

Stephen: Oh yeah, **Taxi Driver**.

John: Where do you think they got that idea?

A reading experience you'll never forget.

TAXI DRIVER

He is a loner. He collects porno pictures. And fares sexy as animals. He carries thousands of dollars in a money belt. And a three-gun arsenal: .44 Magnum, .38 Smith & Wesson and a little palm piece, a .25 Colt. He spends his nights cruising New York streets in a yellow sardine can on wheels. Someone evil is going to die. Someone strange is a hero.

Out of the shadows into the limelight... The terrifying thriller about a night rider... ROBERT DeNIRO in his first role since *Godfather II*

Stephen: Kim is now going to show us a procession, I'm sure.

Kim: I have got a bunch of others that have a similar feel.

Stephen: **Convoy**.

Kim: Yeah, **Convoy**. And this is around that time . . .

Stephen: **99 and 44/100% Dead**

Kim: And this, unusually written by the actual screenwriter . . .

Duane: Alan Sharp!

Stephen: Ah, **Night Moves**, yeah.

Kim: And I suspect this was an influence on Quentin Tarantino, in that the villain's a stuntman.

Duane: *(holding up his own copy of* **Night Moves***)* Awesome.

Kim: And in fact the character portrayed by James Woods is called Quentin. And it's also about the death of Melanie Griffith's character — a starlet. I actually think it's one of the best of the 1970s retro-Noir films.

Stephen: I agree, that's a terrific movie. One of Arthur Penn's last great films.

Kim: Absolutely, yeah. And in this particular context, I would say it's also a great Alan Sharp movie. *Ulzana's Raid* and *Night Moves* — two absolute seminal auteur works which are yet the works of their writer, primarily. And I think in fact Alan Sharp's particular ear for American dialog — he's a Scotsman — it kind of resonates a lot with the way Tarantino writes America. I've just spent a year writing a book about Raymond Chandler, and one of the things that he said was although he was an American — he lived in England until his twenties — he said he had to *learn* American the way that Joseph Conrad had to *learn* English. To him it was always still a foreign language, which is why I think he was obsessed with the

weird little filigrees of it to the degree that a fully American author couldn't be.

Duane: It does take an outside to see the weirdness of your own culture, right? You need someone to parachute in to say why do they speak that way, that's a weird thing to say — I'll put it in a novel and it becomes immortal. Some of the lines out of his gangsters and his low-lifes.

Kim: Yeah. And he kept notebooks full of expressions he heard or found. And I think quite a few he made up.

David: Kim and I are both huge fans of Americans getting Britishisms wrong, and Brits getting Americanisms wrong. Especially in novels, because it's so discordant. But as writers, and we're all writers, you can appreciate that stuff without letting it kick your ass out of the book. And that's relevant to what we're talking about.

Kim: There is a particular thing I like about German Edgar Wallace movies of the early '60s set in London . . .

David: The Krimi films . . .

Kim: It's a version of London that's half the threat in the opera and half swinging London — it's got mini-skirts and 1960s cars but also cobblestones and fog, and it's like yeah, that is the real London, I do recognize it, however nobody lives there.

David: Jack the Ripper is still alive!

Kim: Yeah, and every Soho bar has Klaus Kinski in it.

John: Getting back to the physical format, what did you think, David?

David: I think it fits right in with a sort of a period novelization aesthetic as I understand it. There are two kinds of novelizations in the world — there's the kind that have art done especially for the covers, and there's the kind that tries to collage, in one way or another, existing shots from the movie . . .

Kim holds up the cover to the **Children of the Damned** *novelization by A.V. Sellwood.*

David: . . . based on the theory that I go into in my R&D column (*in this very issue —ed.*) that once upon a time, this was one of the only tangible souvenirs of the movie that you could take home with you. Unless you knew somebody who worked in the movie theater who could score a poster, or unless you tore a picture out of a fan magazine, this was about it. Now, we're swamped in merch, and it's too much. There's too much of it now. Then, if you really lucked out you scored a novelization with a photo section, that was even better.

Kim holds up the **Invasion of the Body Snatchers** *Fotonovel.*

David: And then we get to photo novels, and these were like fumetti for movie people.

Kim holds up the **Can't Stop the Music** *Fotonovel.*

David: Do not evoke that goddamned movie! We had to live with that fucking movie in the Paramount Theatre in the bad old days of Hollywood. The Paramount Theatre was one of our roosts, and we got stuck in there in an apparently endless run of *Can't Stop the Music*.

John: You can't stop the music!

Stephen: There you go. That says it all.

David: You can't stop *Can't Stop the Music*, yeah. It was terrible.

Getting back to **Once Upon a Time in Hollywood** . . .

David But I think it evokes what novelizations used to look like — not in

a major key, in a minor key. I don't know if you felt the same Duane, but when I looked at it I thought, why isn't this a Hard Case Crime book?

Duane: Yep. That, and also, John found somewhere online, someone did a fan art painted cover of what this could be. It looks amazing. Why not use that?

John: It looked even more like **Taxi Driver**, with a painted cover. (*It's by artist Tony Stella. Google it! — ed.*)

David: This would fit on the shelf quite nicely next to **The Nice Guys** (novelization by Charles Ardai).

Duane: Yeah. Completely agree.

David: I've never gotten Shane to confirm this, but I'm convinced that that movie when he wrote it was called *The Bad Guys*.

Duane: I do give Tarantino huge props for having it be a paperback first. That's unusual. He wanted this feel, this format. It feels good. I do love that.

David: It's no accident, is it. The look of the cover, the look of the back cover, and the fact that it's a mass-market paperback original. Quentin has a two-book deal, so there's apparently another book out there, floating around somewhere.

Duane: I think it's a book on cinema, right? More of a non-fiction cinema book, I believe.

Kim: Well there's quite a lot of that in this.

Stephen: Yeah, there sure is. That, and entire chapters on the *Lancer* TV series, but we'll get to that.

John holds up a Lancer *TV tie-in.*

David: (sarcastically) How do you suppose he came to cinema as a topic . . .

Duane: You asked about expectations. Did anyone else expect the ending, the third act of the movie, to be a footnote? That was so weird!

Kim: No, and actually that's the moment when I decided that this book was really worth paying attention to.

David: I love the way that was done. I only fully engaged with this movie during the last fifteen minutes when it goes full comedy, and it's just sort of like, this is so extreme, it's got to be meant to be funny. And I love the fact that the climax is reduced to like a paragraph in the middle of the book. Because another one of the things I love about this book is that it restores Manson to his proper place as a minor, not very interesting guy in history. Manson was a charismatic loser who was railroaded into being the antichrist by a bunch of lawyers. And it's like, he's barely there, and that's kind of as it should be, I think.

Duane: Yeah. I was telling John, if I was hired to write *this* novelization — I'd be promptly fired, by the way.

John: No one else could have written *this* novelization of *this* movie, than Quentin. From my perspective, in terms of expectations, I went in — again, based somewhat on what I believed may or may not have happened with **Kill Bill** — thinking this is a big bite for somebody's first prose novel. And so along the way, I was hit with things like, did he really just squeeze the climax of the film into a flash-forward aside in the most random part of Rick Dalton's day when he's getting ready in the morning? We've now established that's not where this book is going, and I quickly reset my expectations to *this is Quentin Tarantino.* This is going to bounce around in time. This is going to have asides where we're suddenly in a Western. This is gonna have diversions where Quentin's

telling us a Hollywood story. Once I got into that groove, I realized that I was coming at this with the wrong expectations. It's like when people complained about what David Lynch did with the return to *Twin Peaks*; I said, how could you have *any* expectations of David Lynch — other than it being David Lynch and therefore would defy expectations.

David: One thing you'll notice about Quentin's best movies is the fact that they boil down to a series of scenes where people are telling stories to each other. The stories, the asides, the digressions, are like the spokes of a wheel; they always return to the hub. And I think that it's unfair for the people that over-criticized him — *oh, he's not really a writer* — when they're reading the novelization. It's like, this is the guy's first book, okay? Cut a little slack there, friends. And I'm aware of, like John said, the fashion in which he is approaching this subject matter in the book, and I'm willing to forgive a lot in that arena because I know it will coalesce into a bigger thing.

Stephen: On the physical aspect of the book — and Kim, you gave us a very generous showcase of movie novelizations from about 1967 until about 1977 — I come back to you all with this question: what year do you think this film would have come out? And that's kind of my question about what book it should look like. Because I don't think it would look like a book from 1969 — that's when the events happened — so in terms of that aspect I think it's a really handsome package on the book. It looks to me like something from the mid to late '70s, rather than earlier.

David: Steve — It also looks like something that could have been a lot more lurid; it could have had a lot more text on the cover, so therefore, it looks like something intentionally subdued.

Stephen: Well yeah. I respond to the books visually. I'm a writer, but I'm a cartoonist first and foremost, and if you notice some of the books that Kim was holding up, you know in the '60s with the movie novelizations it was almost a stylistic requirement that you took a photo from the movie and slapped a color over it.

Kim holds up the tie-in to **Privilege** *by John Burke.*

Stephen: Ooh *Privilege* — the Peter Watkins film.

Kim: *(referring to the cover)* I think this is a gorgeous job.

Stephen: It is fantastic.

Kim: It's actually better than the posters I've seen for *Privilege* .

Stephen: Yeah. And there was an aspect of movie novelizations from the '60s where a lot of them just slapped the poster for the movie on the cover.

Kim: *(showing off the* **Privilege** *contents page)* Instead of chapters it has a track listing!

Stephen: Oh, man, that brings it to another level! So for me, when I look at and hold the book package, it feels like later in the game; it feels like I've got a novelization for a film that was actually made five to ten years later.

Duane: To your theory, it contains an ad for (Elmore Leonard's) **The Switch**, which came out in the late '70s. You're right — if this is a hint that this book itself is from the late '70s, there's a house ad for a book that didn't exist in 1969.

Stephen: And the first ad in the book as I remember is **Oliver's Story**, Erich Segal's sequel to **Love Story**. I try to go in to any book I read with no expectations. I had read enough novelizations to know that often they have little or nothing to do with the film we're seeing because if they're written from any source material at all, it was usually a first or second draft screenplay — if the writer was lucky to have the access to even that. I also speak as someone who has done graphic novel tie-ins with movies —**1941: The Illustrated Story**, where we actually had to *steal*

the materials for reference that we were working from.

David: And Kim knows that the novelization can also be different depending on what continent you're on. Different versions of novelizations for several movies depending on whether they were written for England or here.

Stephen: Right.

Kim: **The Terminator** has two novelizations. The British one — that came out first — by Shaun Hutson, the guy who wrote **Slugs**. Which apparently James Cameron read, and said we've got to get another one out! I think it's a case that *Terminator* was technically a British film. So it might have been the case that the British distributors just gave Shaun a weekend to write it.

David: It's like that Walter Harris novelization of **Creature from the Black Lagoon**.

Kim: Yeah. The US novelization is by Randall Frakes and Bill Wisher. I'm sure it's a classier read, but I'll bet the Hutson is more collectible.

Stephen: Oh yeah. Going back further Kim, I have two different — maybe it's just the covers, I don't have it in front of me — of **The Man Who Cheated Death**; the Hammer film.

Kim: Yeah, I have a copy of that here somewhere.

Stephen: I don't know if those were the same book with an American cover and a British cover. We all know examples where that varies. So for me, as a reader, I'm in agreement with Kim in that when I was reading the book, I got more interested in the novelization when he buried the climax of the film early, because I immediately went oh, okay, I can *really* let go of expectations now. In a lot of ways, that was for me the main pleasure of reading the novel. Suddenly, Steve McQueen's appearance in the film — which is not in

the book; we don't see Steve McQueen at the party —the running joke of Steve McQueen becomes the punchline of the novel. And Tarantino completely plays that card differently. We have that one sequence in the film where Rick Dalton winces when he's asked by James Stacy. "I heard you almost got cast in *The Great Escape*." It happens *once* in the film, but in the novel, it happens like five times, all to build up to McQueen actually making an appearance at the end of the novel, and we get to enjoy — perversely — the interaction between Dalton and McQueen.

David: What's interesting Steve is that I can't think of another book like that, where having seen the movie is an absolute requisite for your reading the book.

Stephen: You think it's a requisite? I don't think it's a requisite.

John: I don't know how the book could pay off if you don't have the information from the film.

Stephen: I don't know if I would have watched the movie if I had read the novel first. I would have enjoyed the novel, but I would have forgotten it.

David: Do you see it more as a standalone?

Stephen: No, I see them as hand-in-glove with one another. I see them as absolutely bound. But once a book exists, and once a film exists, somebody's going to read this book before they ever experience the film.

Kim: Absolutely.

Stephen: There is somebody out there who is going to read the book first, and the book is about Rick Dalton falling back in love with being an actor. It's almost like a tame version of **The Exorcist** in which the priest regains their faith, if you will. And in the book, Trudi is a far more important character than she is in the film. In fact, I would argue that in the book, Trudi is a more important character than Sharon Tate is. Because Trudi becomes the lifeline for Rick Dalton to regaining his love of acting, which is really what the novel is about.

David: The phone call.

Stephen: Whereas the movie is really about, 'what if'? I can't think of another film, other than the two Leone movies, **Once Upon a Time in the West** and **Once Upon a Time in America**, where having the title at the end of the film had an incredibly powerful meaning to me. Because that's when I realized, this is a fairy tale. Whereas the novel is not that. The novel is really about Rick and Cliff, and it plays completely differently, because in the novel, as you pointed out David, we get the backstory about Brandy the dog. For me, in the film, I don't need the backstory because I see that breed of dog, and I totally accept what happens at the end of that film.

David: As a moviemaker, you can't count on that.

Stephen: Well, you can't count on a lot

of things. You can't count on anybody in the theater even fucking knowing who Sharon Tate is. You cannot count on — in the year 2021 — that any moviegoer is going to make the connection between the longhair who walks up to the house; that he's Charlie Manson. There is nothing in the movie that says to you, *that's* Charlie Manson. That's the baggage *we* bring to the film, and I think the novel functions very differently because Tarantino does give you all that backstory. But you know, I don't like Cliff in the novel. Cliff is a murderous son of a bitch in the novel.

Kim: I agree.

David: He murdered his wife!

Stephen: He murdered five fucking people!

David: He killed five people! He made Brandy do dog fights!

Stephen: He not only murdered his wife, he cut her in half and held her together for an hour until the Coast Guard showed up.

David: I like that Cliff a lot more.

Stephen: I love Cliff in the movie. He is a great fucking character, and when he takes Brandy for a walk, smoking an acid-laced cigarette — first time I saw the movie; tenth time I saw the movie — it puts me in a place that I love to go. Whereas in the book, Cliff is just a dangerous motherfucker.

Duane: On that note, I mean honestly, I wonder how much is that the Brad Pitt factor? Brad Pitt's a charming motherfucker, so in the movie, you can't help but love him no matter what he does. No matter what's going on in his life, it's like, yeah, I still like him. I was all Team Cliff. You're right — in the book, he's a bastard. He really is like a Charles Willeford anti-hero.

Kim: I assume that the Cliff of the book goes on to be Stuntman Mike in *Death Proof.*

(Laughter from the assembly.)

Stephen: Oh yeah, I totally agree with you, Kim!

Kim: That's exactly the direction he's taking. And it's almost like he kills a couple of hippies and gets away with it, a justifiable killing. Who's to say he's going to stop there?

David: Cliff is a serial killer! He's kind of half-way between Brad Pitt in *Fight Club* and Brad Pitt in *Kalifornia*.

John: Duane, I remember when the movie came out, you were one of the ones who was saying, is this guy a sociopath? Is this who that character is? And I think the novel bears that out.

Duane: Totally.

David: By contrast, historically, Charlie Manson never killed anybody.

Stephen: You're right, David.

David: And Cliff is a fucking murderer!

Stephen: But, even there, and this is why I admire Tarantino as a writer — and as a novelist from this book — we get the context of Cliff in the context of Aldo Ray. We get Cliff in the context of Neville Brand. We get Cliff in the context of Lee Marvin. I had forgotten that Lee Marvin story involving *The Spikes Gang*. And those aspects of the novel illuminate Cliff in a different way. It's Rick Dalton who's the alcoholic. Cliff is not an alcoholic. So it actually deepens those characters in a way. What's missing is — and you're right, Duane, part of it is the casting of Brad Pitt — there is one page in the book involving Cliff getting up on the roof to fix the antenna. Now that's one of my favorite scenes in the movie. Just watching Brad Pitt go from putting on a fucking heavy toolbelt — my Dad was a lineman for Green Mountain Power; I know how heavy that fucking shit is — to watch him put it on, leap up on a fence, onto the roof, and casually walk to the peak of the roof is like this sensual aspect of cinema where you buy a character, where you fall for a character, where it becomes pleasurable to watch the character. And I'm not talking about this in a homoerotic way, it's just the pleasure of watching someone that confident, that lithe and limber, in motion. It's like watching Bruce Lee walk in an actual Bruce Lee movie. It's just like — whoah! Or watching Fred Astaire dance in a Fred Astaire movie. And that's gone from the novel, and Tarantino knew he could not translate that aspect of Cliff through the novel, so he didn't even try. He took another whole tact with Cliff.

Duane: That's one of those elements you can't do right, you can't pause and look at a pretty face without over-describing, without purple prose, without interior monologues. You can't just hang with someone and stare at their face in a novel. It's hard to pull off. Those beats of quiet you can do in a movie. So you're right, he realized the limitations of the form.

Stepehen: Right. One of the great pleasures for me in the movie is the dog food.

John: Rat flavor!

Stephen: Right, there's Rat flavor and Raccoon flavor. No, I'm talking about the aspect of just pure cinema of he opens the can and you feel the weight of the tube of shit that falls out of a can. When I first watched the movie it made me laugh; that whole scene with Cliff and Brandy in the trailer was very funny. It's perfectly staged and set up. It works on your unconscious so at the end, when that can becomes a weapon, you totally understand what a dangerous weapon that is. I don't need an explanation of how a human being's face gets caved in with a can of that dog food.

David: Or a phone . . .

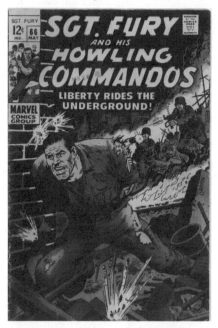

Stephen: I understand how heavy that can of dog food is. And Tarantino the writer — the novelist — gets that, and so he doesn't even put that on the table. He doesn't even clutter the novel with trying to translate that. He makes entirely different choices — that's what works most for me in the novel. The differences are something I really love about the book.

John: Cliff gains a lot in the novel.

David: He gains a rap sheet!

John: Watching the film last night, I saw something that I hadn't noticed previously, and I've spent a lot of time — as Duane I know that you have — examining what's in the background, what books are showing up here and there. When Cliff goes into his trailer, there's a book to the right of his TV set that I hadn't seen before: Shell Scott's **Always Leave 'Em Dying**. Quentin chose for there to be one book that you could clearly read the title of, and it's **Always Leave 'Em Dying**. I thought, how appropriate that came to be for Cliff.

David: Isn't Shell Scott referred to in the novelization?

John: I think there might be an off-hand reference to Cliff reading Richard Prather; not in as much detail as some others.

Stephen: What you don't get in the novel is that he reads Sgt. Fury. And he reads Kid Colt Outlaw. That's a great little thing in the film. For the Cliff in the novel, that's not there at all. We don't know that he's watching Mannix.

To go back to Steve McQueen being suddenly the beat that Tarantino goes to; part of why I respect his writing is he even uses it as the punchline at the end of a chapter to enhance Rick Dalton's character. There's that whole thing about the moustache — which is *not* in the movie — that James Stacey *wanted* to have a moustache for his character and wasn't allowed to by the network. And that the fact that Stacey makes Dalton retell the McQueen story culminates in that chapter ending with Dalton going, "Hey Jim, I was wondering. What do you think of my moustache?" And you know he wouldn't have twisted that knife if Stacey hadn't been a prick. And that's smart characterization; that's smart writing. It's the kind of thing we've seen Tarantino do in his movies, but the fact that he didn't do it in the film and he did do it in the novel was something I really responded to as a reader. He's going somewhere else, and I dig it. This is cool.

John: Watching the deleted scenes again, I noticed that the moustache comes up when Rick is talking with Sam Wannamaker on the set of *Lancer*. It was clearly something that was part of Quentin's reality of this story when he was making the film. The other thing that I thought was fascinating was knowing that he had shot the phone call with Trudi — which Quentin has described as a favorite scene — and yet that the scene was not included with the deleted scenes when the film was released on Blu Ray. After reading the book, I know why he didn't give us that scene.

Stephen: It's the end of the book, essentially.

John: Yeah, he was definitely saving that.

Duane: Totally. It's funny, at the event,

Quentin did a Q&A with a podcast and after a while — and I'm sure it was on purpose — Quentin's own reality blurred with his fictional reality. He referenced Rick and Cliff as if they were working actors. He would start talking about their future films, like, oh yeah, Rick in the '70s, he was doing this and this . . . He had all this backstory in his mind he had cooked up. And I love that we see that in the novelization. We do see a lot of that, which is kind of fascinating. But I do wonder, when you live with something for so long, is there a blur? In the book I love how the young Tarantino shows up. What part of his childhood did he take and amplify in this book, and this movie. It's eye-opening.

David: Having been imprisoned with a fair amount of TV history in my life . . .

(Laughter from the group)

David: . . . I appreciate the level of the detail in the novelization just about the backstory on all those Westerns. And the sidelong hints of what networks were like, what these executives were like, what the demands for changing your character were like; which is really kind of tough to get into when you're trying to fill in the running time in a movie. I am in a position to appreciate a pointed reference to what Jack Lord was like, because *Stoney Burke*, or what Bob Conrad was like, because James T. West.

Stephen: The only important part of that is dealt with in the movie in the first scene with Al Pacino as the agent, Schwarz. Because that's all that's important to set up the story he's telling in the film. Whereas in the novel, he has other concerns. You're right, David, he totally illuminates that. For someone who grew up with all those fucking Westerns, I have to say I OD'd on all that *Lancer* shit.

David: What I'm suggesting is that certain investigations into television have led me to an over-obsession with depth of apparent trivia that I appreciated when it I saw it pop up in the novelization. That part's not for everybody. As I'll admit. As I have found out, there is no bottom to this research.

Kim: In Britain, nobody my age saw *Lancer*. It was on BBC2 at the same time as *Doctor Who* was on BBC1.

Stephen: I have to add Kim, that not too many people in America saw *Lancer*, either.

Kim: But the other shows that are referred to — *The Virginian, High Chaparal, Alias Smith and Jones* — probably were bigger in Britain than in America, because Westerns stayed popular here after the late '50s-'60s boom American in American Westerns. There was a Friday night slot on BBC1 with *The Virginian*. I think that *The Virginian* actually went to a later season where they changed the title to *Man from Shiloh* and brought Stuart Granger in *purely because* of the ratings outside America. And Stuart Granger, a British star was brought in theory to make it more appealing to the country that already liked it. That's why Doug McClure is in those dinosaur movies. Because he was an actual star in Britain, as opposed to kind of a joke in America.

John: As we continue talking about the meat and potatoes of the novel, I want to follow up on something that we've briefly touched on, and David, I want to address this to you first, because one of the aspects of this novel reminded me of some of your work, is the way in which it weaves in Hollywood history. That's something you've done really well in your L.A. based novels and short stories, where you work in this interesting history. I'm curious as to how that struck you in the novel, and also understand what it's like to do that

— to achieve that goal of weaving those elements into your narrative without derailing the story that you're telling.

David: Structurally, I think it's what makes novels interesting; the side roads characters go down. Where one character tells a story to another character. And the challenge — and I think it's a challenge that everybody has faced in the fictional telling of stories or having a character telling a story that is apparently irrelevant to what you're doing, but you hope that it marries up at some future point — is to remember what you were talking about and bring those threads back together. I'm also just very, very fond of, for example, I'm going to mention a Hollywood thing to you. Here are twelve things you probably don't know about this Hollywood thing. You kind of need to know that Hollywood Boulevard wasn't always called Hollywood Boulevard, or you kind of need to know that once upon a time, instead of this glass and steel thing, there was a horrible burger shack there I was fond of called Molly's. If you really want to, you can get a glimpse of it in the movie **Constantine**, because Keanu Reeves grabs a burger at Molly's. It's like that kind of thing. I would imagine that if Kim refers to anything local to London, especially local to the TV industry in London, it has just as much depth and resonance because you don't have to do the research, because you lived through the whole thing. And that's sort of the point of it. You recognize the signs of somebody having done their homework, where in Quentin's case he couldn't have possibly lived through it with an adult perception, so some of it is assumed. But it's a pretty accurate recreation, like you go through a simulation of something and you know what rings as bogus and what doesn't. One of the very things in the book that convinces me of it is the depth of detail that bores Steve so much.

Stephen: I didn't say it bored me, I was sick of *Lancer* is all.

David: There was kind of a lot of it, yeah.

Duane: To me, that's the main attraction. Before I was a writer, I was a fan. David, reading your stuff was my way of traveling to L.A. without being here. Those side stories were everything. And Kim, in the Kim Newman-verse, all those connections you make — it's like, this is what I'm here for. It's wonderful; those side trips.

David: I also think it impacts you differently if one is a transplant to L.A., having grown up with a set of notions about Hollywood derived from TV and movies, as opposed to actually pounding the turf. Also, Duane started out as a journalist, and so even when you're reading prose you become vitally concerned with the who, what, why, where, when aspect of it, and if it's not there you feel its absence.

Duane: Totally. You can feel someone glossing over it, too. We mentioned before about when British writers try to do American and vice versa. Like James Hadley Chase, a famous example of tough guy fiction. It doesn't feel like America at all. It feels like a weird ether of all these tough guy movies. It's kind of fun, but . . .

Kim: Tarantino talks a lot about Karl May, who's a weird enthusiasm of mine — the German Western writer who I think did visit America later in life after he became a successful novelist. He wrote all his wild west stories without going anywhere near America.

David: Here's the thing, though, Kim — in this book in particular, and speaking of what we were just talking about — you definitely get the feeling that Quentin didn't just Google this shit. He didn't get his references off Wikipedia. He didn't get his film timelines off IMDB, you know what I mean? He knows the stuff from the ground up, and it's apparent.

Stephen: Did any of you have issues with some of that stuff in the novel?

Kim: There was nothing I could see that was factually off. It did strike me strange how some of the internal monologue where we're getting what Cliff thinks

about movies did not sound like Cliff; it did sound more like Quentin.

Stephen: I agree. That's why I'm asking.

Kim: But there were some moments where Cliff was thinking things, and I was thinking, no, Quentin wouldn't think that. He's trying to subtly suggest — for instance, although it's funny — I think that whole riff about Sharon preferring The Monkees to The Beatles makes sense. She probably would be able to relate to them more. They're from her background; it's her culture. But it's an unsupportable argument!

(More laughter from the group)

Stephen: This is something I struggled with. I was framing an interstitial for a project called **Studio of Screams** and I had to figure out what I had to leave in to create a fictional movie studio that was convincing. When I was reading **Once Upon a Time in Hollywood**, I thought why is it the one movie that it's possible Rick Dalton *might* have seen — in fact it was shown on the CBS late movie before what happens in the film happens — why does Quentin not recognize *The Fearless Vampire Killers* as the only movie where any American would have seen Roman Polanski's face and Sharon Tate's face on the big screen. And he buries it in the novel. He refers at one point to the poster being in Sharon's house, which we barely see in the film, so it's something he thought about, oh, I've got to mention this in the novel. And that's a point where I go, oh, well, okay, Quentin doesn't think much of *The Fearless Vampire Killers*, but as a writer that shouldn't have been an issue for him. He should have used that device. That is a powerful narrative device for a novel set in America, with a protagonist, Rick Dalton, who doesn't like foreign movies — and even hates Spaghetti Westerns! That *that* would have been why he would recognize even who fucking Roman Polanski was or even looked like! That was the point where I saw Quentin's prejudices as a film lover — as a film devotee — getting in the way of

Quentin the novelist dropping what would have been a perfect shorthand storytelling device. I'm not looking for him to love *The Fearless Vampire Killers* . . .

Kim: Or *Dance of the Vampires*, as we call it . . .

Stephen: With the proper title, as Kim has pointed out, *Dance of the Vampires* . . .

David: Not the edited version . . .

Stephen: But it's the edited version that played on the CBS late night movie; that *was* available — I mean I saw it on 16mm film at film society showings in fucking Northern Vermont! That's one of the points where after finishing the novel I thought, huh, he really kind of dropped the ball there. He could have used that.

Kim: Does he even mention *Eye of the Devil*?

Stephen: No. That's not even mentioned. And *Eye of the Devil* was on television as well.

Kim: I admit that it's not a film that's particularly well known even now. It kind of keys into the themes of this novel, in a way. I assume that it's the film Sharon Tate made outside America aren't of particular interest to him.

Stephen: That's fine, but those are the ways that an American would have recognized Sharon Tate. And that's definitely the way an American in 1969 might have visually connected — oh, Roman Polanski and Sharon Tate are an *item*, right? Because it wasn't until Sharon Tate was dead that any Americans were seeing photos of Roman and Sharon in *Life Magazine*. I mean, I was buying issues of *Films and Filming* and *Sight and Sound* magazine as a teenager, and *I* didn't connect Roman and Sharon except because of *The Fearless Vampire Killers*. And I don't mean to dwell on it, I'm just saying, as a writer, I go — there was a perfect tool for you to use, and you didn't use it. It would have been a deft way of making a connection that's important to the novel.

Duane: What's funny is that I think Tarantino actually *is* a fan, because I went to an all-night horror comedy at the New Beverly, it's actually called "Quentin's Horror Comedy Night," and he hand-picked these six movies, and *The Fearless Vampire Killers* was one of them. By the way, you haven't seen *The Fearless Vampire Killers* until you've seen it at 3AM, exhausted and jacked up on Diet Coke. That was surreal!

David: Are you recommending this?

Duane: I am! Watch it at 3AM, jacked up on popcorn and Coke!

Stephen: I'm going to do it tonight!

David: We should actually have a Zoom about that!

Stephen: There were also points where I was sort of relieved that Quentin didn't shift into that gear. He gives a little background about the New Beverly Cinema, and he refers to it as Slapsy Maxie's, and I breathed a sigh of relief of, oh good, there's not a paragraph about who Slapsy Maxie is.

David: Max Rosenbloom!

Stephen: Exactly! That was an invitation there that he chose not to take.

David: He appears in *I Married a Monster from Outer Space*.

Stephen: He's in *The Boogie Man Will Get You*.

Kim Newman: Having just written a Hollywood novel, one of the things I did in the editing process was cut out a lot of that stuff. Reading this book I got a sense that maybe Quentin didn't have the kind of editor that I had, who *will* come in and say stuff like, yeah, this is all very interesting but could we get on with the story . . .

David: No, in fact, Kim, Quentin could bust us on this, but I don't think he was edited very much at all for this.

Stephen: And going back to the reference point I made, he cites *The Fearless Vampire Killers* three times in the novel. I think that's why it jumped out to me by the end, saying, man, why didn't you use that. I mean, three times. Use it once to make the visual connection.

John: My sense, David, was who at Harper Perennial is gonna say, "Quentin, let me tell you how to tell a story . . . "

David: Yeah, "Can you cut out Trudi's phone call, because it's kind of boring . . . "

John: The one thing that he did mention in several interviews was that one editorial note he got was they felt that Cliff kind of disappears towards the end of the book. And that's why the Aldo Ray chapter got placed where it did; so that there was a last bit of Cliff towards the end. Once they get to the Drinker's Hall of Fame, Cliff is there, but he's not really involved because it's the actors sharing their stories.

Stephen: We're not even told that Cliff killed all but one of the people who attacked the household! That's not mentioned at all. If you just read the novel, you'd think that Rick Dalton had killed everyone who showed up at the house.

David: That suggests there's kind of a **Fight Club** thing going on here . . .

Stephen: Well, it also suggests to me that the Cliff we see in the movie *is* the Cliff we see in the book. I mean, what's the first thing he says in the movie, yeah, I carry his load, that about sums it up. And at the end of the movie, with one line, he's driven away in the ambulance, same thing.

David: Cliff is Tyler Durden. Actually Rick killed everybody and is blaming it on an imaginary stunt double.

Stephen: Right. Cliff's just like, aw, fuck it.

Duane: So Rick is his own stuntman, then — he's his own double. That's fascinating, right? Okay.

David: One of the things that Quentin mentions in the book is Cliff's disdain for guys not only like Bruce Lee, but Bob Conrad. Bob Conrad — the first *actor* ever admitted to the stuntman hall of fame. Because he loved getting in fights so much; but I completely believe Cliff's attitude — yeah, you let a lot of stuntmen take it on the chin for you.

Stephen: Because of research on a different project I just read that fan book that came out about *The Wild, Wild West,* and that's pretty accurate to what Bob Conrad was doing on *The Wild, Wild West* set.

David: The Susan Kesler book.

Stephen: That's it. And I also remember reading all the articles in *TV Guide* when *The Wild, Wild West* was on, and I have no problem buying that Bob Conrad might be on a stuntman's shit list. There were other prejudices that Quentin had that played differently in the novel. Because he buries the climax of the movie, the references to 'those dirty hippies' do not play in the novel as anything except Quentin pushing that button. I mean once it got to that point in the novel, Trudi even has a line of dialog where she says — you know, an eight year-old girl — "Just for me, I find hippies . . . kinda sexy . . . kinda creepy . . . and kinda scary." And it's like, where's that coming from? That has nothing to do with Trudi's character. And that's one of the points where I'm like, okay, Quentin doesn't like hippies. I got it. By the way, there are three or four hippies *right here* in this panel, I'll point out.

Kim: I suspect that a film he probably *doesn't* relate to is **Alice's Restaurant,** which for my thinking, is that era encapsulated.

Stephen: Well he does make the reference in the novel, Kim, that even Arlo Guthrie is an actor.

Kim: Yeah, that's true.

Stephen: It makes sense when he has the reference to Dennis Hopper. I love that line in the novel that Rick Dalton is "an

Eisenhower actor in a Dennis Hopper Hollywood." That to me is the perfect one-sentence description of Rick Dalton as a character. Whereas in the movie, it's when Dalton comes out with the iced margarita and he's got the robe and he hammers his fist on Tex's car and says, "Hey! Dennis Hopper, move this piece of shit!" That's a reference in the novel very different from its use in the film, but it resonates. That played true for me in a way that the dirty hippie lines did not, because they don't matter any more with the climax not being the climax. It's a different story now.

Kim: So, what kind of a career do we think Rick Dalton has after famously killing people?

Stephen: Aren't we given a procession of the movies he's in, or am I misremembering?

Duane: We are. We have a flash forward of a few of the roles he has after that.

David: Didn't he make like four Spaghetti Westerns?

Kim: Yeah, but that's during the period covered by this narrative.

David: Oh, right.

Kim: You never get a sense of how basically killing some home invaders affects his career.

Duane: That's true.

Kim: Because he would be a tabloid name.

Stephen: Oh yeah, for sure.

Kim: He would be someone famous for that.

RICK DALTON

NEBRASKA JIM

REGIA SERGIO CORBUCCI

TECHNICOLOR® TECHNISCOPE®

Stephen: That means he would be cast in *Death Wish*, right?

Kim: *Death Wish* perhaps. Probably *Walking Tall*, first.

Stephen: Yeah! You're right!

David: That means he would be Chuck Connors.

Kim: Yeah, except because he's Leonardo DiCaprio's size, he *couldn't* be Chuck Connors.

David: Well no . . .

Stephen: He couldn't be walking tall, either, Kim . . .

David: He would be Nick Adams!

Kim: Yeah. That's who I thought he was in the film. It struck me that maybe he should have gone to Japan and made those monster movies.

(*More laughter from the group*)

David: This is particularly poignant because Quentin has a movie theater at his house and once I went over there and I watched Quentin's print of *War of the Gargantuas*.

Stephen: Brad Pitt's favorite movie, as a matter of fact.

David: Yep!

Stephen: The weird thing is, you're right Kim, we're not given that. I had printed out from the novel, the one career that we get a flash forward to is Trudi Fraser. Quentin puts her in all kinds of movies.

Kim: She's sort of not quite Jodi Foster.

David: I always saw her as kinda like Janina Faye.

Stephen: Here's where he puts her. "She was nominated for an Academy Award three times. The first time was in 1980 when she was nineteen and she received a best-supporting actress nomination for playing Timothy Hutton's sort-of girlfriend in Robert Redford's *Ordinary People*." And her second best supporting actress nomination was in '85, when she was Sister Agnes in *Agnes of God*.

Stephen: Yeah, we don't get anything for Rick Dalton, do we.

John: I've got a theory about that. This is something else that Quentin has talked about. He had the book deal for two books — the novelization and his cinema book. He has said that he has written **The Films of Rick Dalton**.

Duane: Yes, he did say that.

John: One of those classic books that details an actor's entire career. I really hope he publishes it, because it would be fascinating to read the detailed history of Rick's career.

David: There is a site called Nestflix.com, and it's got a page for each of Rick Dalton's movies.

Kim: Incidentally, I looked it up and it was Elizabeth McGovern and Meg Tilly who played those roles.

David: Well yeah, without the Academy Award nominations Trudi could have been Elizabeth McGovern.

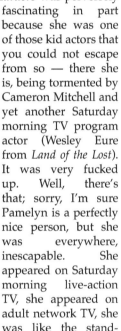

Kim: I'm not sure if Elizabeth McGovern was a child actress. Scrolling back through her credits, no, she wasn't.

Stephen: As someone who grew up with the television that this novel and this film involves, if I hadn't seen the film I would have pictured Pamelyn Ferdin when I read Trudi's character in the novel. Because Pamelyn Ferdin was that child actor you may remember; she was the girl in *The Beguiled*, the Don Siegel film, who has the turtle.

Kim: And *The Toolbox Murders*.

Stephen: *Toolbox Murders* was perversely fascinating in part because she was one of those kid actors that you could not escape from so — there she is, being tormented by Cameron Mitchell and yet another Saturday morning TV program actor (Wesley Eure from *Land of the Lost*). It was very fucked up. Well, there's that; sorry, I'm sure Pamelyn is a perfectly nice person, but she was everywhere, inescapable. She appeared on Saturday morning live-action TV, she appeared on adult network TV, she was like the stand-in, surrogate, late-'60s American kid that you found abrasive if you were a kid in America.

Kim: She played Lucy on the Charlie Brown animations.

Stephen: I rest my case, Kim! I rest my case.

(*More laughter from the group*)

Kim: I'm just looking at her credits, and you're right. She was on *Gunsmoke* and *Star Trek*. And *Custer* which is actually mentioned in the novel.

Stephen: That's right.

Kim: And *The Legend of Jesse James*.

Duane: Excellent casting! You're right. Damn.

Stephen: But because I saw the movie first, of course I picture Trudi from the film. Had I read the novel first, being the age I am and the background I have, I would have pictured Pamelyn Ferdin. That's the voice I would have heard, and I would not have liked her character at all.

Duane: Hey guys, who would you have cast, based on the book alone, to play Cliff Booth?

Stephen: Good question.

Duane: Cause that's a whole different character to me. It's not Brad Pitt. In the '60s-'70s, who could pull that off.

Stephen: It would have been Andrew Prine.

David: A much younger Scott Glenn. Like, *Gargoyles*-era Scott Glenn.

Stephen: Yeah, but Scott Glenn . . .

David: Actually, Scott Glenn *now* could do it . . .

(*More laughter from the group*)

Kim: I always think of Andrew Prine as Simon King of the Witches. He was a hippie, not a . . .

David: Did you ever see that photograph of J.K. Simmons where he's completely ripped from working out in the gym?

Kim: I know who I would cast as Cliff Booth *in* the '60s — Tim O'Kelley from *Targets*.

Stephen: I would argue Gary Busey.

Duane: Gary Busey, that's interesting too.

Stephen: Or . . .

Kim: You know Gary Busey was playing pacifist hippies in *Angels Hard As They Come*.

Stephen: Yeah right. That's why I'm picturing him. Actually, it probably would have been William Smith . . .

John: Yeah, I was going to say William Smith becomes the natural choice . . .

Stephen: William Smith as Cliff, right?

David: William Smith is a good pick.

Stephen: He's dangerous. He kills people. And you would be afraid of him.

John: 'He's too pretty to be a stunt man.'

Duane: And Cliff is pretty . . .

Kim: William Smith did a lot of those roles where he came on and lost fights. He's in the *Rockford Files* pilot as the guy James Garner beats up.

John: Garner tricks Smith . . .

David: That's right, he sends him flying right into a urinal.

Kim: He tricks Bruce Lee in *Marlowe*, as well!

Stephen: And don't forget, William Smith was on *Rich Man, Poor Man*. That was a big breakthrough role for him.

Duane: That's good.

David: We are getting lost in this forest . . .

Stephen: We are . . . One of the things I wanted to mention with the novel about Cliff — I did love the aspect of Cliff being a ringer. That Cliff would be the stuntman that stuntmen would get on the set to punch Otto Preminger out one time. Or to kick Bob Conrad's ass one time.

Duane: That was cool.

Stephen: That was completely believable, and made him a little more endearing.

David: And to speak to the earlier question, there was nothing in the book that struck me as discordant, from what John asked much earlier. There was nothing in the book that kind of hangnailed out at me as being an obvious, no, that's wrong. But then again, I only saw the movie once; I only read the book once. So if I did a deep dive, I might find some other things.

Stephen: The only thing that jumped out for me as a hangnail was the sentence about *Repulsion*.

Kim: Yeah, you're right.

David: What about it?

Stephen: *Repulsion* played in America as an exploitation movie first, and then had a longer life on the art house circuit and as a 16mm film. When *Repulsion* opened it had a really nifty one-sheet poster, which I have, but it was sold as a psycho film.

David: Didn't art house people see *Knife in the Water* first, anyway?

Kim: Absolutely.

Stephen: Yes, definitely. But *Cul-de-Sac* never took off in America. But when you asked about a hangnail, that one sentence about *Repulsion* is where I just went, that's not quite what happened. But it's okay, it didn't pull me out of the novel.

Duane: The Brandy stuff didn't trip me up in the novel, but it was a lot meaner and darker . . . the movie left me with, oh, it's a sweet man and dog story. But it got really dark. It's like *Cockfighter* all of a sudden. It's like holy shit!

Stephen: Yeah, and he kills the co-owner!

David: I have a question in general. Something struck me about this, and again it's the difference between the movie you would make, and the movie Quentin would make. Is there anything about this

story that you would have told differently in the novel or in the film?

Stephen: I think the movie's perfect.

David: I'll give you the reason I ask this question, because I thought, how much more powerful would it have been if we hadn't seen Sharon Tate in the movie at all — until the very end, and she's just a distant figure that walks out in the driveway and says, "Hi, I'm Sharon." And that would have broken everybody's heart.

John: I think because I didn't have enough to build her into a character, I enjoyed those early scenes — as frivolous as they may have been — just getting to see her *alive*. Living, smiling, laughing . . . being this kind of quirky, funny character. I think if I hadn't had that, her surviving this story would have resonated differently. I know that one of the complaints that a lot of people had with the movie was that they felt Sharon had nothing to do in the movie . . .

Stephen: That's not true, actually. Sharon, in the movie and the novel, is the only nouveau riche character we see who interacts with a hitchhiker on a human level. Everybody else in the novel and in the film — we never get a sequence like that chapter in the novel; and it's a short sequence in the film, but we see she has a pleasant conversation with the female hitchhiker she picks up and drops off. That for me was the fulcrum of the importance of Sharon's character in the narrative. She was the one nouveau riche character who was not caught up in the class struggles we see all the other characters caught up in on different levels. I mean, let's face it, Rick Dalton is caught in a class struggle. He wanted to be a big Hollywood star, and we're catching his story when he's on his way down. And Cliff, that's not even a factor, but his career hinged on riding the coattails of Rick Dalton, a character on his way up, who is on his way down. And we see the bottom feeders; that's what the whole Spahn Ranch sequence is about. Sharon to me is important. I don't need a lot of time with her, David; I think I get what you're saying. But I need enough time with her to see that it was possible for somebody to move freely in L.A. without all the baggage that we see all the other characters carry. And if that makes her flighty, or lightweight, I get it. But that's also why her character is important. Does that make sense?

Duane: Yeah, I agree with you, Steve. I really think if we had that, she'd just be a cipher, and I wouldn't care anywhere near as much as I did at the end of that movie.

David: I think she's still a cipher. Yes, she's one of the Beautiful People, and what befell her was a tragedy that defined an era . . . but that doesn't make her a talented actress, or even culturally worthwhile. I've been to her grave at Holy Cross — it's near Bela Lugosi's grave. I only ever recognized her from *Dance of the Vampires*. But I always saw her as more or less about the same temperature as Dorothy Stratten.

Duane: Yeah, but I saw her being happy and joyful. It's like she's a star who's ascending whereas Rick is a star who's descending. She was the one character where any kind of hopes you have for a beautiful career; those are on her, right? You don't want to be anybody else in that movie. You want to be her.

John: And because they build that up, because she's on this rise — for those of us watching the film thinking, we know the trajectory of her story — it's like there was this hope, this aspiration, and we know it's going to get snuffed out. But when it doesn't . . .

Kim: Is it deliberate that the other Hollywood people we see are Steve McQueen, who died young – as did Bruce Lee and Mama Cass; Roman Polanski, who the entire rest of his life was mired in scandal; and James Stacy, who crippled himself in a motorbike accident a couple of years later. These are all people whose success did not last. Strangely enough, Roman Polanski is the most long-lastingly successful of them all, and he's an international fugitive!

David: Also, all of the grief in the story for every character that I can see derives from show biz. Even Manson's desire to be a rock star.

Stephen: Well wait a minute. I would also argue that Sharon is the only character we see who has no apparent aspirations, is not climbing on other people, and who is the only character who we *briefly* get to see her enjoy celebrity. And what she enjoys is that she is entertaining other people. It's completely guileless. This makes her a cipher, I agree Dave, on that aspect, but I also think it makes her the only likable character in the movie in a way.

David: What about Trudi?

Stephen: We don't know about Trudi. I *love* Trudi in the film, and I don't know if I would have liked her in the novel because I would have been . . . I'm *sorry* Pamelyn Ferdin — please understand that I am simply talking about the face and voice that was inflicted on me on television. You're right about Trudi. But Trudi is a character, who in a way, is illuminated by Sharon's character, because we can see that there is a possibility of functioning in this entertainment world without becoming a toxic person.

Kim: Everything I've heard about Elizabeth McGovern says she's a perfectly nice person and an enormous talent who has managed to sustain a career without actually becoming a huge star. But has done consistently good work at every age range she's been in.

Stephen: I think you're right, and we *need* that in this story. That archetype you're talking about, Kim.

John: Did Trudi's scenes in the book change anyone's opinion of her?

Duane: She is more of the emotional heart of the novel, whereas in the movie she's almost a fun aside; a quirky little kid, wise beyond her years. It was amusing, but I couldn't really say that I took to her character, and thought about her much in the movie. The book is very different, though. She is the future. She is the heart of the book.

David: In the book she's more clearly one of the mechanisms of any potential redemption that Rick might have.

Duane: Which is interesting in an uplifting way. In the same way the movie had that sort of lightness of heart — oh my god, this world isn't that fucked up and bad — the book had that in a different way. She provided that emotional response in the novel.

Stephen: Her moment in the film, which becomes the climax of the novel, that dialogue between her and Rick Dalton happens 92 minutes into the movie; halfway into the film. And transposing that relationship to being the grace note that the novel ends on completely reconfigures everything just the way you described, Duane. If I ever got to meet or talk to Quentin, that would be my question for Quentin the writer — what was the reason for shifting that. Because the movie has a very different focus, and a very different grace note that it is heading for. And in the novel, Trudi is the only redemption for Rick.

Kim: I find Trudi entertaining; I don't find her all that convincing as a child. She strikes me more as a shaman figure. But then again, who knows what Jodie Foster was like at that age.

David: Uh-huh. As much as I detest "sage children" characters, I think Kim's right. But her value is earned, whereas we're just supposed to accept Sharon Tate's goddess status because she's one of the Beautiful People.

John: It's interesting, because in the film, the character works because of Julia Butters' performance.

Kim: Oh yeah.

Duane: Absolutely.

John: It's like Duane was saying, it's an interesting aside. It's amusing and entertaining, but she's certainly got more weight in the novel. I thought it was funny when she was pushing Rick's buttons and he called her a little bitch. It had me thinking that I'd *really* like to see those scenes they shot, because I want to see how those played out between Leo and Julia.

David: Yeah, I want to see more of what they shot.

John: I'm sure we will, eventually. It will come out in some way, shape or form.

Stephen: The strongest words they trade in the movie have to do with him calling her 'little pumpkin.'

John: 'Little pumpkin-puss.'

Stephen: And she has that great comeback, where she not only puts him in his place, but also says, "I can see you're upset, so we'll talk about this later."

John: And you just *know* that she will . . .

Stephen: Yes, she will!

John: It's not like we're *not* going to talk about this; we're just not going to talk about it *right now*.

Stephen: Someone had asked earlier whether there was anything that pulled anyone out of the novel. Being a writer who's also worked in comics, show don't tell is a real basic tenet for me. And the Manson chapter — the chapter with the creepy crawl into the house — I get why he did it. I don't have the experience that all of you here have as novelists, particularly Kim and David — I bow to you both.

David: Stop groveling!

Stephen: The Manson chapter was the one that kind of stuck out like a sore thumb for me, because it suddenly became tell, not show. He was *telling* me who Manson was. And because Manson's not important to the novel, it stuck out even more for me after I finished it; so like why did we need that backstory.

David: By the same token, the creepy crawl is a scene I would have *loved* to have seen in the movie.

Stephen: The creepy crawl scene worked; it was the lead-in to that chapter. The show-don't-tell function stopped, and suddenly we're getting this download of information. I've gone through the same pains when I'm writing short fiction. There will be something where I'm like, I've got to get this piece in here, and I'm not sure how or where to put it, and it suddenly becomes clumsy exposition.

David: Where you crash headlong into the info-dump.

Stephen: And that was the only point in the novel where I felt that. I don't know how the rest of you felt.

Duane: I remember a magazine writer talking to us when I was a young journalist working on a magazine. They said good journalism is actually a good use of show *and* tell. It's two pedals. You *show* when you want people to feel something; you *tell* to deliver information. You use both. Showing is not any better than telling, it's just how you use it back and forth. I didn't mind it as much. Some things need to be sped through; I don't need to hear everything in detail. But I do see your point, that was a little weird. It also changes Pussycat's character. She was very sweet and delusional in the movie, but she's sinister in the book. She's really a fucking monster.

Stephen: She was masturbating in Cliff's car!

Duane: All right, sweet in my own way. That's my definition of sweet, I guess.

(More laughter from the group)

John: As Steve pointed out earlier, the film, unlike the book, is really about the 'what if.' How do you think the American culture would have changed based on the events of *Once Upon a Time... in Hollywood* in 1969?

Kim: A thing that *Yesterday* – the film where a protagonist travels to an alternate timeline where the Beatles weren't a successful band – blithely ignores is that there would be profound consequences of taking something as culturally significant as the Beatles off the table. No Beatles (no Richard Lester), no Monkees – no Monkees, no *Easy Rider* . . . no *Easy Rider*, no movie brats . . . no *Jaws*, no *Star Wars* . . . no MTV . . . and so on. That's just pop culture, let alone fashion, politics, language, haircuts, religion, world events. Plausibly, a Beatles-free world of 2019 would be unrecognizable to us.

So, no Manson murders . . . Maybe the dominant image of hippies remains *Hair*, despite the concentrated efforts of the Establishment to demonize peace protesters or the Black Panthers. Maybe the Woodstock vibe and the summer of love continues . . . Nixon doesn't get re-elected. Roman Polanski makes *The Day of the Dolphin*, which derailed Mike Nichols' career when he made it . . . so *Chinatown* goes to, say, Arthur Penn. Do Roman and Sharon stay married? – odds are against it, but who knows? Polanski married two other actresses – one (the *Werewolf in a Girls Dormitory* chick) didn't last but he's been with Emmanuelle Seignier for years. Sharon would never have been his Tess, but he might have found something else to make with her (the most Sharon-like star he worked with in the 1970s was Sydne Rome – maybe Sharon would have been sweet and funny and sexy in *What?*). Looking at the careers of the other young women who were in the Matt Helm movies or *Valley of the Dolls* and comparable introduce-new-faces films like *The Group*, it has to be said that Sharon Tate was among the least distinctive – she'd not have been in the frame for the kind of 1970s movies that Jane Fonda, Karen Black or Faye Dunaway starred in, and I suspect she'd have found it hard to land roles if her competition was Janice Rule, Katharine Ross, Cybill Shepherd, Stella Stevens or Jessica Walter. I can see her guest starring on *Banacek*, or maybe landing a TV series – *McMillan and Wife* or *Police Woman* (though, still, Susan St James and Angie Dickinson just have more personality than Tate got to show in the films she did make). But, considering a no-Manson timeline might have been sunnier, maybe bright and smiling Tate in a tailor-made comedy vehicle would have been the screen face of 1970 rather than Jane Fonda in *Klute* or Karen Black in *5 Easy Pieces*? I do wonder how much of the darker tone of Hollywood in the 1970s was influenced by the Manson murders – we can think of a couple of obvious items (*Count Yorga Vampire*) that draw on Manson, but maybe even *The Exorcist* (which is about a terrible invasion of the home of a famous actress) would be off the table as not quite on a non-Manson-universe's timeline. Other factors – Vietnam, civil rights clashes – were in play and key horror films (*Night of the Living Dead* and, of course, *Rosemary's Baby*) were pre-Manson, so the progress of that genre was already set . . . but maybe Wes Craven would have remade another Bergman (*The Face, Hour of the Wolf*) for his horror film rather than gone down the evil hippie home invader rapist killer cult guru path with *The Last House on the Left*. In the novel, there's a moment where Sharon picks up a hippie hitchhiker and the narrator says that a year later because of how she died someone like her would stay away from a hippie – taking that out of the equation might have made for a different outcome of the culture wars. That said, Manson wasn't the only longhair giving hippies a bad name – I grew up near Glastonbury, and there were 'no hippies' signs in cafes . . . I met open, kind, thoughtful, creative folk from the counterculture . . . and also exploitative bastards who were in their own way trying Manson's exploit-the-followers act. Without Manson, there'd still have been Jim Jones.

Stephen: Wow. Yes, well, hey, having grown up with plenty of beloved hippie friends and all, they're just people: good, bad, lovely folks, twisted fucked-up assholes, every shade in-between. We'd already had a procession of 'bad hippies' on TV and in movies pre-Manson, and thanks to the Cowsills, we still had the cleaned-up fictional The Partridge Family and squeaky-clean Osmond family making the long-haired lads wholesome post-Manson as it is, didn't we?

But I think there were two major speculative carry-aways for me, which were very different from how the novel had me feeling. The movie really had me wondering what life would have been like had the murders never happened, period. I hadn't really pondered that; it's a transformative notion, transcendent, even.

So, first carry-away: Might *2001: A Space Odyssey*'s Star Child have won the zeitgeist in the long run, instead of the Anti-Christ of *Rosemary's Baby*? As Kim suggests, maybe *The Exorcist* — and, barring that existing or taking off, then no Damien of *The Omen*, and so on — just wouldn't have seized the public imagination as it did and still does.

Oh, I'm sure America would have invented the boogeyman that was needed, but it might not have been a Charlie Manson. Manson really supplanted Aleister Crowley, "The Beast," in the popular culture — completely replaced him — fulfilling a projection that must have been essential for it to so dominate where the culture and counter-culture went by 1970. But had there been no such murder spree, had Manson and the Family never been noticed, never existed as far as the public was concerned, where would the 1970s have gone? Sans Manson, would the intensive and long-overdue self-scrutiny initially triggered by the November 1969 revelations of the Thảm sát Mỹ Lai, the Mỹ Lai massacre, have not been so handily usurped and swept under the carpet? Those horrific photos of the massacre aftermath shot by U.S. Army photographer Ronald L. Haeberle were shocking, but the media blasted them offscreen (as it were) with the horrors of the Tate–LaBianca murders. Would C Company platoon leader Lt. William Calley Jr. become the 'projection screen' Manson so quickly became? We'll never know. After all, Manson wasn't actively murdering anyone — Calley was and did — but we'll never know. The only artifact of the pop culture I've ever found that tangled with the conflation of the "Charlies" (Charlie Manson, Lt. Calley's

Charlie Company) was Tom Veitch and Greg Irons's underground comic *Legion of Charlies*, which is essentially forgotten today.

But I'll just leave my sad little hippie-dippy notion out here: without the Tate–LaBianca murders, would the **2001** Star Child been the face of a new generation? Would that have persisted, grown, supplanted what we ended up having?

Second carry-away notion: Might there have been other positive outcomes without the caricature of Manson eclipsing Calley, Nixon, and so on? Might we, as a culture, as a nation, not taken this steady swing to the Far Right, to what we've become? Without Manson, without the murders, would Nixon have become the boogeyman? Would we have ever had a Ronald Reagan Presidency, or two Bush Presidencies, or Donald Trump being anything except a failed real estate broker? Would we have had **Star Wars** to so radically sterilize and revitalize a new generation embracing war? Would the lessons we should have learned from Vietnam been learned? Or would we have just manufactured a Manson surrogate regardless, and would the rest have fallen into place as it has anyway?

I'm otherwise completely in agreement with Kim. I'll take that a bit further: in a recent interview, Barbara Parkins talks about how the murders "changed the way that Hollywood lived. Movie stars before that time had no home security, but that all changed after the Manson family murders."* This also transformed Hollywood product, leading to a fresh fetishizing of police, extreme security measures, firearms, home defense, etc. The unsolved Scorpio murders combined and conflated with Manson led to Andy Robinson's nameless killer in **Dirty Harry**, and the "my, that's a big one" fetishizing of Harry's Magnum. Would we have had the relentless fetishizing of firearms in Hollywood films and TV without the Manson murders? Maybe yes; I mean, Don Siegel was making films like **Madigan** and **Coogan's Bluff** before the Manson phenomenon (and don't get me wrong, I love Siegel's films), but the Manson murders fundamentally changed Hollywood — the point, entirely, of **Once Upon a Time... in Hollywood**, the movie — and that reconfigured and deformed Hollywood product on a primal level, too, and thus the nation and the culture.

Instead of speculating on the possible pop culture that might have followed, look, there's a kind of speculative science fiction I love deeply, and **Once Upon a Time... in Hollywood**, the movie, embodies that; it prompts me to inhabit that. The only other recent reading experience that does this for me is Luke Kruger-Howard's graphic novel **Goes** (2021), specifically the chapter entitled "Men's Holding Group," which propositions a single cultural shift — what if men were kind to one another? — and shows us an alternative future based on that one shift. That's what the film **Once Upon a Time... in Hollywood** does, but Tarantino's entire elaborate construct simply, elegantly, pops the question: "what if?" Over and out — here, you go live with it, see where it takes you. As with **Yesterday**, the speculative ripple effects are incalculable.

The difference is, unlike **Yesterday**, Tarantino just leaves us with that notion, that potent grace note, to carry with us. It's a great 'What If?' that resonates — and it's not at all what I carry away from the novel. Hey, really, I'm awfully glad Dalton falls back in love with acting, but the movie had and has me seeing potentials I just haven't had any other movie or novel in recent memory spark.

John: It's funny that the thing that resonated for me most in **Yesterday** was the one key difference they did reveal about that world. And it wasn't even about the scene, or what happened in the movie; it was just the fact that sitting in the theater, we saw John Lennon alive, and I suddenly stopped to appreciate the fact that this was a world in which he lived beyond 1980. I do think that primed me for the emotional impact of Sharon surviving that August night in 1969.

Of course, as a child of the '70s, I grew up with the image of Charlie Manson as

* Barbara Parkins interviewed by Anthony Petkovich, *Shock Cinema* #60 (2021), pg. 12.

boogeyman (thanks in large part to Steve Railsback's performance in **Helter Skelter**). And Manson didn't do anything to change that image through the years. I can't begin to imagine who or what might have filled that void had Charlie been all but erased from history.

As for Sharon, while the odds of her having a successful acting career may have been remote, even when relegated to the worst-case scenario for her cinematic future, I *can* appreciate that she still would have lived to experience it.

David: I'm still grooving on the concept of the ability to erase the Beatles footprint, because I was never a fan of their vapid pop, which is today's supermarket Muzak. But my family moved to Huntington Beach in 1966. I distinctly remember living right next door to hippies, about the time I was watching first-run *Man From U.N.C.L.E.* episodes, in our house on Dublin Lane (what is now Drew Park used to be a tomato field next to our house, at the end of the block).

These individuals had a zebra-striped van. Tie-dyed home-made drapes. They played a lot of guitar on the porch. Colored lightbulbs. But the important part was that they weren't hurting anybody by existing alternatively. I think they were actually renting the house from the owner, who lived in a cottage out back, wore these enormous muu-muus, and drove all over town in a golf cart. But suddenly my neighbors weren't from prime time TV, you know – the fake nuclear family fallout from the Gray Flannel Suit era, the early 60s.

I was 13 years old in 1968, 14 in '69. I was buying *Famous Monsters of Filmland* at a place called Hilltop Liquor, which apparently still exists on Beach Boulevard. I was definitely hitchhiking to get around by then, and there was none of the pedophile or serial killer vibe that's omnipresent, now. More often than not you'd get into a great conversation during the ride – the kind of conversation you couldn't get from your family or parents, the kind you could get from the odd-but-not-essentially-different people living right next door.

Hippies in movies? Nothing remotely close to what I saw in real life, until **Easy Rider**. "Real life," of course, being permanently conflated with "movie life."

Stephen: Do any of you think if this novel had come out first, that there ever would have been a film version?

Duane: In the real world, yes, because Tarantino would make it. I do wonder how people respond to the book first, and think, what the fuck is this? Without that payoff.

John: I don't think he would have written *this* book, and published *this* book, before making *that* movie.

Kim: I'm trying to think of comparable examples. Unlikely books by filmmakers that they then turn around and film. Maybe **The Big Red One**. Usually what happens is filmmakers become novelists because they can't get green-lit any more.

David: Or as we have seen, there are a great number of novels out there that started life as screenplays.

John: And that's my point. I don't think — and I think Quentin has said as much — this isn't so much a novelization of that screenplay. This is a very deliberate alternate approach to what exists as the film.

David: There would be room on the bookshelf for a straight novelization of the movie that would go right alongside this.

Kim: I remember seeing Nigel Kneale interviewed at the time of the **Quatermass Conclusion**. And I remember the little 'ugh' in his expression where he said, "I'm writing it as a novel. Not an (ugh) novelization."

(More laughter from the group)

David: The word itself is automatically reviled from square one. It was automatically looked on as a trash form of literature and they existed like 100 years ago. There were novelizations of silent movies.

Kim: There were novelizations of plays. **Peter Pan** was a novelization. Probably **The Third Man** is the highest literary form novelization. It's kind of a screen treatment rather than a novelization, but it is a prose work by Graham Greene based on the screenplay.

Duane: I was wondering if you guys ever read a novelization before seeing a movie. In my household, my parents weren't paying for many movies in the theater. I can count on one hand the movies we saw in a theater. But I was hungry to be part of that conversation, so I encountered *Alien, Clash of the Titans*, even **2001** in book form first; before seeing the movies.

Kim: I remember, because they were a staple paperback of the '70s, I read **Tales from the Crypt**, the novelization, before I saw the film. Stuff like **Countess Dracula**, and I've got the Hammer Horror Omnibuses. I think several of those I read before I was old enough to be allowed to see the films, or before the films were on television. I don't know at what point that stopped.

the soundtrack LP before I ever got to see the movie.

Duane: Oh yeah. Exactly.

Kim: There were also instances like *Queen Kong* where the movie never actually came out, but the novelization was around. One I particularly remember because it took a long time to get any release in Britain was *Dark Star*. Alan Dean Foster did a brilliant novelization of **Dark Star** which was around in Britain years before we could see the film. I remember so many films where I read the *Mad Magazine* satire before I saw them.

Stephen: You're right Kim. Definitely.

Kim: Particularly films like *The Exorcist* or *Dirty Harry*. All those movies were X certificate at the time, so I couldn't see them for a couple of years. But I could read "Dirty Larry" and "The Ecchorcist."

Stephen: I remember buying novels thinking that they were movie novelizations. Joe Millard was writing the Spaghetti Western novelizations, but then they continued The Man With No Name, and I was looking for those *other* movies! **A Coffin Full of Dollars** . . . And it was like, oh, there never was this movie.

Stephen: David, you made the reference earlier that novelizations were the only sort of artifact you could take home from a movie, and that wasn't entirely true. What people forget is that movies used to open either in the cities — it would take months before they would reach us in the sticks. Or if it was a rural film, we would get to see it before it played Boston or New York. Movies didn't used to open everywhere day and date. That didn't become a phenomenon until 1975 with *Jaws* and 1977 with *Star Wars*. Typically I would read a novel, a comic book, and listen to

Kim: They were another instance of the peculiar way that the Westerns stayed current in Britain after they faded in America. I believe a lot of those Joe Millards were commissioned by British publishers.

Stephen: You're right.

Kim: It was New English Library who had published the Richard Allen skinhead novels, and they also published the Robert Lory Dracula novels. They specialized in those 120-page pulp nonsense which were playground favorites. I've also got Joe Millard's **The Hunting Party**.

Stephen: I've tracked down every Joe Millard I could find. And good luck finding them today. He's one of those authors who has just disappeared from the shelves completely.

Kim: I've got a bunch of the Dollars books . . .

Stephen: And **The Gods Hate Kansas** . . .

Kim: I have that, but I don't think that was ever published as a tie-in to *They Came From Beyond Space*.

Stephen: No, you're right. There never was. I was thinking, I had the novelization of **Color Me Blood Red** years before it would have been possible for a kid to see the movie.

David: There were also legitimate novels that were made into movies that published what they used to call movie editions . . .

Stephen: Yeah, I've got a lot of those.

David: . . . where they would have some promotional art from the movie on the cover.

Stephen: **Mysterious Island**.

David: Yeah. **Lost Horizon**. I always bought novelizations compulsively, but I never recall doing anything like what Steve is talking about — where he got the novelization and the soundtrack beforehand, prior to the experience of actually seeing the film. I would never listen to a soundtrack LP before I saw the movie. But I completely understand the circumstance. I bought plenty of novelizations for movies that I had not seen — and never would see — just because they were movie books, in a period where there weren't a lot of movie books.

Stephen: Right. I think I remember reading Jerome Agel's **The Making of 2001** before the movie reached Vermont.

Duane: That's what I read. I devoured that book, and learned everything about the movie before I saw it years and years later. I have it on my shelf. It's an incredible book; essays and behind the scenes stuff.

Stephen: It's a brilliant book.

David: The same thing happened to me. My parents went to see *2001* when it opened. It was a special showing at the Chinese Theater. I know because the tickets were so expensive — they were five bucks each!

Stephen: Big bucks back then.

David: And my stepmother made my father leave fifteen minutes into the movie. I had heard it was this terrific movie, and she comes back and says, no, it's just a bunch of apes jumping around.

(More laughter from the group)

Stephen: What's wrong with that? That's my kind of movie!

David: So like Duane, it took me another decade to see the fucking movie. So in that case, yeah, I went to the book first — but the book had prior resources, like the short story.

Stephen: I read the paperback of Peter Watkins' **The War Game** long before it was possible to see it in America. It was the same book designer that had done **The Medium is the Massage**, so it wasn't packaged not as a novelization, but images juxtaposed with verbatim text from the film. That was a case of the book was the *only* way to experience in any form what the movie was.

John: Now that Quentin has entered into this new arena, where would you like to see him go as an author of prose fiction? Personally speaking, there are aspects of some of his films that I think might be interesting to see given a similar approach as to **Hollywood**. I'm not necessarily interested in seeing this kind of diversion for *all* of them, at least not as interested as I am in seeing something original. Of course if he chose to continue the **Kill Bill** story in novel form as opposed to a film, I'd certainly be interested in that.

David: I think this should stay unique.

Duane: I wouldn't mind seeing **Double-V Vega** — the novel. Unrealized projects.

David: He sure has the notes . . .

Duane: I'd rather see it, and if it sucks, so be it. It's out there, at least. I'd rather see a failure than to not see anything at all. I do hope he has more truly original novels. Like truly original, and not on the shoulders of a movie, that he can bring out at some point.

David: Oh yeah, I'm all for that. Sure. Because the more Quentin waffles about the remainder of his film career, whatever that turns out to be, he could expound to his heart's content in book-land, and he's already got a built-in audience that loves his obsessive approach.

Stephen: I read Kim's **Anno Dracula** books, and I see those as the movies Kim would make if he had a studio convinced to do it. And I'm also the editor that told Tim Lucas, as a writer — when his concept for **Throat Sprockets** was derailed because the

cartoonists who were drawing the work did not want to continue — that it was his property, and he should just do it as a novel. And we wouldn't have the novel **Throat Sprockets** if there hadn't been that path. If this is the beginning of a different path in the creative life of Quentin Tarantino, hey, I'm on board as long as I'm alive and can read. That's a no-brainer for me.

David: Based on the experience of reading this novelization, I would certainly pick up whatever came out next.

Kim: Yeah, I'll certainly read his stuff. One thing that's actually quite unusual is that he's not exactly a prolific filmmaker. It's not a huge body of work to get your head around; now with one piece of associational material. I always thought in his case the tie-in soundtrack albums were sort of an important ephemeral, or additional way of experiencing his properties. They feel very curated. They mostly have dialogue snippets as well, although I can't remember if **Once Upon a Time... in Hollywood** does.

John: It has the KHJ radio bits.

Duane: In college, the **Reservoir Dogs** soundtrack was constantly playing in every dorm I walked past. That was a true soundtrack hit in addition to this culty crime movie. And **Pulp Fiction** actually kickstarted a whole marketing thing of pulp fiction. You know what I loved to see this time? People were rabidly hungry to get this book. And I don't see people eagerly seeking out a book anymore. It was nice to see that. That you have to celebrate.

John: It's funny that Kim was talking about the music. At one of the last theatrical screenings of **Hollywood** I went to, I brought in a notepad because I was working on assembling, in the correct order, a track-by-track soundtrack of all the needle drops — all the songs, the cues from the trailers, ads and TV shows — to try and build out an ultimate soundtrack album, because I knew the released album would only contain a fraction. I think I've probably got 60 tracks.

Duane: I did the same thing. I have a playlist with 50 songs versus the twenty on the album.

Kim: The playlist for the novel would be much longer, because it includes stuff like The Beatles, which you couldn't get. It's not quite true for this period, but one of the things that's true of all films set in the 1960s — they under-represent The Beatles, because securing the rights to their songs is difficult. I genuinely remember walking down a street in 1965 and hearing a different Beatles song coming out of a succession of places. They were inescapably pervasive. Films about The Beatles don't get it right. Even *Yesterday* only sprang for like 18 songs.

Stephen: When you talk about the music, one of the things that's been characteristic of every Tarantino film is the selection of music — whatever function it served in the film — was always familiar to me, but it was not a Top 40 number. But I knew it. I recognized it. Even look at the film we're talking about. He doesn't choose the Paul Revere and the Raiders song that we did hear and see all the time on the radio or on television. He chooses one that's familiar, and it hits that sweet spot.

Kim: It does have "The Circle Game" and "Mrs. Robinson" though . . .

John: Yet "Mrs. Robinson" is cut off just as it gets going . . .

Stephen: Exactly.

David: I'm so glad that they didn't put that "Snoopy and the Red Baron" song in the movie.

Stephen: And yet they did!

Duane: They did though.

David: They did?

Stephen: He's listening to it in the pool.

John: He's singing it!

David: I don't remember it. I've blocked it out.

Stephen: You've blocked it out . . .

David: Now that I've mentioned the damn thing it's going to become an earworm again.

Stephen: I'm hearing it right now. Thank you David.

Kim: I used it as the title of a novel.

(More laughter from the group)

Stephen: The one thing I'll say in answer to your question is if we are seeing a transition in terms of Tarantino's future creative path; if novels and writing books is going to become what supersedes making films, you're right, there's only what, nine movies?

Kim: Yeah.

Stephen: That's a solid body of work; there's nothing wrong with that. But given how difficult it is to make one fucking movie in America right now . . .

Kim: And he is remarkably privileged. I'm trying to think of another wide-release film that's as daring and experimental and personal — and *not* part of a franchise. Unless you think that Quentin Tarantino is himself a franchise.

David: He's his own IP.

Stephen: The last time we had an American filmmaker in that position was Oliver Stone. The period when he was making stuff like *JFK* and so on. People would go because it was an Oliver Stone film. And then *that* went away, too.

David: That is so last century, Steve.

Stephen: Well hey, I said the *last* time, David. It will be interesting to see *if* this becomes a vehicle for Tarantino, what is that going to be. Will we be looking at a time where there's a new Tarantino novel, and there's a CD soundtrack we can buy to listen to while reading the novel.

David: It will be a book/CD combo, but nobody does hard media anymore, so it will be hard to get the CD.

John: Well he has said that he has written a play adaptation of **Hollywood**. I for one would be interested in seeing it, just to see his approach.

Stephen: If there's any media that's harder to access than cinema right now, I would say live theater is it.

David: He could've done it as an opera.

Stephen: You know, "Snoopy and the Red Baron" would be a great aria, Dave.

David: Or as a ballet.

Kim: This isn't material I would necessarily see as congenial for the theater. Having worked in the theater, I think it's a really fascinating art form, but this isn't a theater idea.

John: Not like **Reservoir Dogs**.

Kim: That's absolutely a theater idea.

Kim: Unless he wants to do a whole play which is just Rick and Trudi talking.

Duane: That's true. That's a funny thing — he always confounds expectations. Walking into the movie, I thought, okay, it will be a Manson thriller kind of thing — it's nothing about that hardly at all. It was great. I could imagine Cliff and Rick at the Smokehouse in Burbank — that's the entire play. Just talking about killing a pig. The whole thing could be just that; a microcosm of this larger world.

Stephen: I could go to a play that was just the agent, Schwarz, meeting with his clients, one after another.

(More laughter from the group)

Duane: That would be great.

John: He said that when he needed to figure out something about Rick's character, he would just start writing it out as a conversation with Marvin. I could totally see that as a play.

Stephen: Marvin is such a great character. Pacino just inhabits the role.

John: Whatever path Quentin chooses to take from here, I think it's safe to say that the five of us are all ready and willing to go along for the ride. Anyone have any parting thoughts?

David: I don't really have a summary statement to offer so much as an observation, and maybe a question for Quentin. Firstly, it's weird for me to see Leo Di Caprio and Brad Pitt as these mega-star types because I first encountered Brad Pitt when he was slumming on *Freddy's Nightmares*, and Di Caprio's first feature film was **Critters 3**. Of revisionist speculation, Chuck Palahniuk, who wrote **Fight Club** (the novel) once said, *"Let Jay Gatsby leap from the pool and grab the gun."* That is, let Gatsby become proactive about preventing his own murder, and turn the tables on the person who comes to kill him, not because he's Jay Gatsby, but because the killer has mistaken Gatsby for the man who ran over his wife (in Gatsby's car). Of course in the most recent film version of **The Great Gatsby** (2013), Di Caprio plays Gatsby. And in **Once Upon a Time... in Hollywood**, when Sadie invades Rick's home, it's not to harm a specific target so much as anyone who happens to be inside. So my magic question for Quentin would be: Is the whole swimming pool climax a hat-tip to **The Great Gatsby**?

That's all I've got, folks, and thanks for coming!

FANTASTIC COMICS OF THE SILVER SCREEN
Genre Film Comic Adaptations
by William Schoell

The fifties and sixties were a ripe time for films of the fantastic — science fiction, fantasy and horror — and the comic book companies responded with special tie-in editions that kids in particular would be interested in. There were earlier comic book adaptations of movies, of course. Some of these, such as *Hollywood Film Stories*, used panels from the movies while others were illustrated. *Movie Comics* (Picture Comics) featured a downright bizarre, caption-heavy combination of both stills and artwork. One of the earliest films adapted for comics was ***One Million B.C.*** in 1940 in Whitman Publishing's *Crackajack Funnies* 25 and 26. It was abbreviated and not especially memorable.

Fawcett comics, most famous for Captain Marvel, came out with a tie-in to the George Pal production of ***Destination Moon*** in 1950; this was based on the novel by Robert A.

Heinlein, who co-wrote the screenplay. The film detailed the first trip to the moon in a rocket with four men aboard. Once they arrive, they realize they used too much fuel on landing and may have to leave one man behind to stabilize the rocket's weight so they can take off. Fortunately, they figure out a way to get rid of the excess weight without anyone being left behind. Fawcett's comic version is almost as good as the movie, with a solid script by comics legend and sci-fi writer Otto Binder and pleasant, efficient artwork by Dick Rockwell and Sam Burlockoff — although it's a shame that they don't provide a full-page shot of the striking lunar landscape as seen in the film. The comic shows much more of the home life of scientist Charles Hargraves, introducing us to his three young sons as well as his wife. (Of course the fact that Hargraves has children makes it even stranger that he's willing to sacrifice his life when they discuss who will stay behind.)

A Fawcett Publication

approaching the earth, and a strange visitor who arrives on the moors in a spaceship — is he friend or foe? Because the science in the movie is so ridiculous — the earth would probably be destroyed by another planet coming that close — it makes a perfect 1950's comic book, and even has art by Kurt Schaffenberger, a prominent DC artist of the period and later. Otto Binder did the script, adding a few details and sequences — a deputy is terrified by the appearance of the alien and dives out of a window — and giving the alien a musical language that no one can understand. Schaffenberger's work is professional, even attractive at times, but not especially dynamic. Like *Motion Picture Comics,* most of the movies adapted in *Fawcett Movie Comic* were Westerns.

Dell and Gold Key were especially prolific when it came to movie adaptations, with Dell taking the lead in sheer quantity. Dell's comic adaptation of Walt Disney's 1954 **20,000 Leagues Under the Sea,** based on Jules Verne's classic novel, is almost as entertaining as the film version. Paul S. Newman's script follows the movie closely. Frank Thorne's art is reasonably effective, if undistinguished, but it does pull the reader along at a fast pace. None

Binder's script also adds interesting scientific points during the voyage that are not in the movie.

Fawcett's *Motion Picture Comics* 110 presented an excellent, reasonably well-drawn (by George Evans) adaptation of the film **When Worlds Collide** in 1952. This was the story of desperate efforts to build a rocket ship to take forty people off the earth just as it is destroyed by a star from another galaxy; the ship will land on a planet that is orbiting this new star. As the day of departure nears, there are outbreaks of violence and resentment from those who will be left behind. The comic went the movie one better by depicting the final explosive destruction of the earth, which is never shown in the film, although this is only seen in one small panel. Larger panels showing the destruction of New York City by tidal wave, volcanic eruptions, and people falling into giant cracks in the earth are more impressive. The script by veteran comics scribe Leo Dorfman was primarily composed of dialogue from the movie.

Another 1952 release, **The Man from Planet X,** became the feature in *Fawcett Movie Comic* 15. (This was a separate series from Fawcett's *Motion Picture Comics.*) The movie deals with a planet rapidly

of the characters resemble the actors in the slightest.

Dell then came out with a poor adaptation of *The 7th Voyage of Sinbad* in 1957 which completely lacked the excitement and wonder of the excellent original. Gaylord Du Bois' script eliminates the fight with the animated skeleton at the end and future Marvel superstar John Buscema's art job is not one of his better ones. (In 1975 Marvel comics did its own adaptation of the movie in *Marvel Spotlight* 25 written by John Warner and drawn by Sonny Trinidad. It was not appreciably better than the Dell version.)

Dell's *The Land Unknown* (1957), about an expedition to the South Pole that searches for a patch of warm weather and discovers a lost land of prehistoric monsters, was almost as exciting as the movie. Beautifully rendered by gifted artist Alex Toth, the comic boasted a couple of spectacular half-page panels, one depicting a Tyrannosaurus rex advancing on a helicopter as it takes to the air, and another a monster rising from a lake and capsizing a make-shift raft. The monsters in the film, aside from some real-life lizards, are mechanical beasties with limited movement, but Toth, while maintaining the basic look of the creatures, gives them a more fluid and attractive

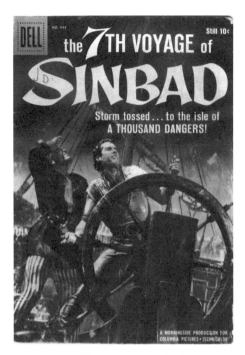

appearance. The characters in the comic approximate the look of the actors without resembling them that much; the male characters all tend to look alike. The comic added a couple of extra touches such as the heroine nearly being grabbed by the claws of a lizard and almost being popped into its mouth. Robert Ryder's script compresses some scenes and dialogue in an intelligent fashion. In the comic the character of Dr. Hunter, who tries to assault the one lady in the group, apologizes for his actions which he never does in the film. The film makes clear that marriage is in the cards for the romantic couple but this is not made as certain in the comic.

Hercules (1958) was an Italian mythological epic starring Steve Reeves that was dubbed and heavily promoted in the American market. In this Hercules tries to clear his old teacher of the murder of a king and help his son, Jason, take his rightful place as ruler. To that end Jason, Hercules, Ulysses and others travel to Colchis to regain the golden fleece, which was stolen years before. *Hercules* is an entertaining if minor adventure flick and the Dell comic was about on the same level, although the only resemblance between Steve Reeves and Hercules in the comic was that they both had a beard. The script by Paul S. Newman actually fills in some of the gaps in the movie's continuity and makes the relationships between certain characters much clearer. The art was by John Buscema and it's clear that he was destined for greater things, although his work would become much more striking in the future. Buscema, unfortunately, depicts the dragon who guards the fleece almost exactly as it looks in the film, and as the movie's dragon is a rather pitiful specimen, that's not a good thing. Otherwise, it's a nice job.

Dell came out with the comics version of the sequel, *Hercules Unchained*, in 1960. *Unchained* is somewhat better than *Hercules*, with a more interesting story, as the demi-god becomes involved in a war between two brothers, sons of Oedipus, both of whom want to rule Thebes. Much of the film takes place on the island of Lidia, where a kidnapped Hercules — who has lost his memory due to inadvertently drinking the "waters of forgetfulness" — has been taken to become the latest plaything of Queen Omphale, who memorializes all her murdered lovers by preserving their bodies. Hercules manages to get away with the aid of Ulysses, but his disappearance blitzkriegs a truce between

the aforementioned brothers, and a full-scale war breaks out in an exciting climax that features the brothers fighting a literal duel to the death.

As he did with the previous film, Paul S. Newman crafted an excellent script for the comic version, again clearing up some plot points and establishing relationships that were a little fuzzy in the film. Newman adroitly compresses events so that the comic is actually better-paced than the movie. The art is by no less than Reed Crandall, and it is generally attractive work, if not necessarily his best. Crandall and George Evans inked over Crandall's pencils. Hercules looks like Steve Reeves, and the other actors are also well-delineated.

Dell released an adaptation of the film *Journey to the Center of the Earth* in 1959. Written by Robert Schaefer it eliminates some unnecessary scenes such as the kidnapping of Alec (Pat Boone) but also jettisons such scenes as the giant boulder that nearly crushes the adventurers, the caverns of crystal, and worst of all, the sequences with prehistoric animals, including the Dimetrodons on the beach and the giant red lizard that attacks at the climax. This is strange, because Verne's novel *did* include the monsters (as well

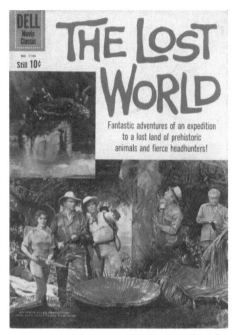

as a giant humanoid shepherd). The script incorporates much of the film's dialogue and pulls the reader along in an entertaining fashion, but the art by John Ushler is pedestrian.

Dell's *The Lost World* (1960) was a fair-to-middling adaptation of the second film version — produced and directed by Irwin Allen — of Sir Arthur Conan Doyle's classic novel of modern-day man finding dinosaurs on top of a plateau in South America. Paul S. Newman's script follows the movie closely and makes few changes. The penciling was done by comics legend Gil Kane, but it is not the artist's best work and one might have trouble at first even recognizing it as Kane. The problem may have been the inking reportedly done by Mike Peppe. The comic had two improvements from the film: it made the giant arachnid who menaces a native girl a trapdoor spider with big eyes that emerges from the ground instead of dangling unconvincingly from an overhead web; and the strange disembodied tentacles that bar the entrance to a cave and are rather pitiful in the movie are shown as long, sinuous and very dangerous appendages in the comic book. The poodle that accompanies Jill St. John everywhere on the plateau is eliminated. Some of the

characters in the comic resemble the actors. The name of big game hunter Lord John Roxton is inexplicably changed to Ruxton with a "u."

Another 1960 Dell movie adaptation was *Dinosaurus!* In this two frozen dinosaurs, a Brontosaurus and a Tyrannosaurus rex, along with a caveman, thaw out and cause havoc on an island. Two men, Ward and Chuck, overseeing construction on the island, do their best to save pretty Betty, a little boy, and the other residents from danger. The script by Eric Freiwald and Robert Schaefer follows the film closely, but completely eliminates the character of Chuck aside from a mention in one word balloon. Also excised is a scene when the Tyrannosaur crushes several people inside a bus. With its mediocre artwork by Jesse Marsh, the comic is roughly equivalent to the motion picture with its poor models and crude stop-motion effects.

Dell also adapted *The 3 Worlds of Gulliver* in 1960. The film detailed our hero's adventures in first Lilliput with its tiny citizenry and then Brobdingnag with its colossal inhabitants, and had more-than-decent effects by Ray Harryhausen. Paul S. Newman adapted the script and employed a great deal of the movie's dialogue. The pencils were by Mike Sekowsky of *Justice*

53

League of America fame but it was not one of his more memorable assignments, a rush job that hardly displays his mastery of composition. Mike Peppe's inks did as little for Sekowsky as they did for Gil Kane in his **Lost World** adaptation. The comic does not compare favorably to the motion picture, although the sequence when Gulliver wakes up in the giants' doll house with his fiancée is handled more dramatically than in the movie.

The Sword and the Dragon was a 1960 dubbed American release of a creditable 1956 Russian fantasy film called *Ilya Muromets*, the name of the story's hero. Ilya is a farmer who is given a special sword and sets off to aid his king by fighting an evil despot and his minions, which include a three-headed, fire-breathing dragon. Dell's adaptation was an excellent and faithful rendering of the movie with some very nice art attributed to Jack Sparling in some sources, but which looks a lot more like John Buscema. Leo Dorfman did the script, which eliminates such moments as when four warriors get impaled on one spear, although the scene when the despot orders all of his constituents to climb on top of one another and form a living mountain *is* depicted.

Dell's final 1960 movie adaptation was

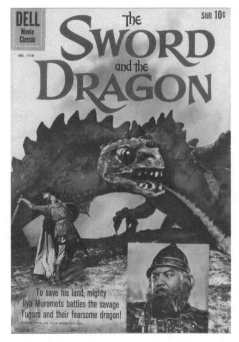

of George Pal's **The Time Machine**, which depicted the hero's adventures in 800,000 A.D. where the human race has divided into the cattle-like Eloi above ground and the cannibalistic Morlocks beneath the earth. The uncredited script for the comic follows the film version closely, and there is respectable art by Alex Toth, although it might have been better if Toth had let someone else ink over his pencils. The comic book is unable to capture what is the highlight of the film, the time-lapse photographic effects that create the illusion of time travel for the viewer.

Dell's adaptation of Jules Verne's **Mysterious Island** (1961) was a near-perfect encapsulation of the film, in which some Civil War soldiers are trapped on an island inhabited by gigantic animals. All of the monsters — a giant crab, a big testy bird, economy-sized bees, and a mean-tempered squid — are depicted, albeit briefly, and the uncredited script incorporates much of the film's literate dialogue. Tom Gill's artwork is clean and efficient. (Herb Trimpe inked the backgrounds while Gill embellished the main figures.) In the comic the exchanges between Captain Harding and reporter Spilitt over the morality of Captain Nemo's

actions, such as destroying war ships and all hands aboard, are eliminated, with Nemo simply presented as a man who seeks peace. The characters do not much resemble the actors in the movie. Dell also came out with another adaptation of Verne's novel — *Jules Verne's Mysterious Isle* — in 1964 that was more faithful to the book, which had no monsters at all.

Atlantis the Lost Continent was a 1961 George Pal production in which a fisherman named Demetrius takes a shipwrecked princess back to her native land of Atlantis and discovers that the evil powers behind the throne are building a destructive, laser-like weapon with which they hope to conquer the world. Dell's comic book version in no way measures up to Pal's very entertaining movie. Although he later emerged as a significant talent in the comics industry Dan Spiegle's art — he both penciled and inked — is disappointing, although there are a couple of effective half-page panels depicting a volcano blowing its top and the giant laser running amok. The comic eliminates the scene when the mutated beast men turn against their creator, and although we see evil Zaran and the sanctimonious priest being blasted by the super-weapon, they are not instantly skeletonized as in the

movie — a nifty touch and an early shock for kid viewers. There is no attempt to make the characters in the comic look anything like the actors. A sympathetic character played by Jay Novello only appears briefly in the comic. The serviceable script was by Eric Freiwald and Robert Schaefer.

Dell's version of *Voyage to the Bottom of the Sea* came out in 1961. This was Irwin Allen's attempt to duplicate the box office of both *20,000 Leagues Under the Sea* and *Journey to the Center of the Earth*. This story of a fantastic nuclear sub, the Seaview, going on a mission to save the world when the Van Allen radiation belt catches fire, was one of Allen's best and most entertaining pictures, but the comic adaptation just doesn't compare. Sam Glanzman's standard penciling is not well-served by his own inks. There are numerous small changes in the (uncredited) script and one major change. Instead of a gigantic octopus attacking the sub just before the climax, the comic has a gargantuan sea serpent — "ten thousand times the size of a boa constrictor" and with a maw big enough to swallow the Seaview whole — wrap itself around the sub and start to drag it into its lair just as another serpent comes along to try to get it for its own supper. I can only imagine

55

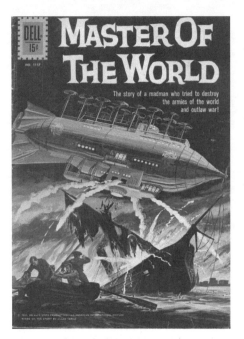

that kids who read the comic book first were sorely disappointed when they saw that this scene — which might have been a knock-out — doesn't actually occur in the movie. Stars Walter Pidgeon and Peter Lorre are well-depicted in the comic.

Another 1961 Dell movie adaptation was *Master of the World*, loosely based on two novels by Jules Verne, with Vincent Price playing a variation of Captain Nemo — only in a heavier-than-air flying machine instead of a submarine. Gaylord Du Bois' script follows the basic plot of the film but uses little of the screenplay's dialogue, and even makes some changes along the way. The two men who are rivals for the heroine come to an understanding in the comic, something that never quite occurs in the movie, for instance. Jack Sparling's art is serviceable and no more.

Gold Key's *Captain Sindbad* (1963) featured attractive art by Russ Manning but writers Eric Freiwald and Robert Schaefer made quite a few changes from the movie. Sindbad comes back from a long voyage hoping to be reunited with a beautiful princess, but discovers that the land has been taken over by a tyrannical dictator, El Kerim, who is impervious to death because his heart is protected in a great tower in the middle of a deadly swamp. The first half of the comic follows the movie faithfully, but the second half — although the main plot is the same — adds sequences that were not in the film, either the inspiration of the comic's writers or sequences that were in the original screenplay but were never filmed (or left on the cutting room floor). In the comic the hydra the men face is replaced by a minotaur and a chimera. In the comic Sindbad and his men are beset by giant ants that at the end are magically transformed back into 8000 missing men — none of this occurs in the finished film. Sindbad and El Kerim do not have a battle on the top of the tower as in the film, and the comic's ending is a bit abrupt. Overall, it does not compare that favorably to the very colorful and exciting motion picture.

Jason and the Argonauts was released in 1963 and this story of a search for the golden fleece amidst a variety of deadly perils emerged as one of the finest fantasy films ever made, and is perhaps Ray Harryhausen's greatest achievement. In addition to the wonderful effects work, the movie is classy on every conceivable level: Bernard Herrman's musical score, production values, costuming and art direction. Alas the Dell comic version is vastly inferior to the motion picture. Paul

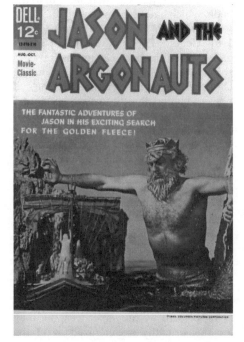

S. Newman's script is mostly faithful to the screenplay aside from a couple of relatively minor deviations — Jason is forced to go on his voyage because of threats to his sister and Hermes takes Jason to Olympus in a chariot — but penciller John Tartaglione seems little inspired by the wealth of mythological material. Dick Giordano's and Vince Colletta's inks can only help so much. Scenes that crackle with excitement in the movie are comparatively pallid in the comic — the scene with the many-headed hydra is a little better than the others.

The film adaptation of H. G. Wells' **The First Men in the Moon** came out in 1964 and that same year Gold Key came out with the comics version of the movie. Unlike Wells' novel, much of the film is very silly and it takes nearly an hour for three voyagers — scientist Cavor, playwright Bedford, and Bedford's fiancée, Kate — to make it to the moon in their sphere coated with a gravity-defying substance. The adventurers discover a lunar society of busy, scuttling insect-like creatures inside the moon along with gigantic moon cows that resemble out-sized caterpillars. Paul S. Newman's script for the comic is well-done, although it eliminates the sub-text of

Bedford introducing the "selenites" — as the moon people are called — to violence over an appalled Cavor's objections. The rest follows the movie very closely, and this includes the prologue and epilogue that take place in modern times (astronauts discover the Union Jack on the moon!). The art by Fred Fredericks is only slightly better than serviceable. The moon men and moon cows look pretty much as they do in the movie, and the characters are at least the same type as the actors although they only resemble them superficially.

Also in 1964 Dell released a movie tie-in of Roger Corman's Poe pastiche *The Masque of the Red Death*, arguably the best of Corman's collaborations with Vincent Price. The sadistic Prince Prospero invites a fair young lady — along with her father and boyfriend — into his castle for his own evil amusement even as the plague of the Red Death ravages the countryside. Meanwhile a dwarf plans a diabolical revenge against a lord who dared to strike his little lady friend. The uncredited script follows the film closely and doesn't soften Prospero's horrific actions and character, although it eliminates the scene when Prospero's lover, Juliana, is slashed to death by a falcon's claws (a sequence that sort of falls

needs to be operated on — from *within* his body! Paul S. Newman did the script for this, omitting the sub's voyage through the inner ear and the subsequent attack of anti-bodies on the curvaceous Raquel Welch, and giving the sub's inner journey the name of Operation Lilliput. The film is a wonder to look at, with its incredible sets and art direction and special effects that still hold up even though this was years before CGI. The look of the comic is not on the same level, however, although Dan Adkin's pencils are not bad and they are inked by the combo of Tony Coleman and no less than Wally Wood. Whatever its flaws, the comic adaptation is still quite entertaining.

In 1968 producer Ivan Tors came out with an imitation of *Voyage to the Bottom of the Sea* entitled *Around the World Under the Sea*. In this a submarine transverses the globe underwater so that the crew can put seaquake warning sensors on the ocean bottom. There are a variety of minor dangers, including an alleged "attack" by a giant moray eel. The Dell comic, written by Paul S. Newman, follows the story almost exactly but eliminates the unconvincing romance between two of the characters. It is actually a bit more enjoyable than the rather bland movie version. Jack Sparling

flat in the movie, anyway) and tones down the death of the aforementioned lord. Frank Springer's artwork simply covers the action in a very uninspired manner, although the comic is still a good read.

Dell released a tie-in comic for the Boris Karloff film *Die, Monster, Die* in 1965, and it was essentially as mediocre as the movie. The film was a loose and inferior adaptation of H. P. Lovecraft's masterful novella "The Colour Out of Space," and focused on the strange effects of a glowing meteor on people, animals and plant life. The hero does his best to get his girlfriend, a member of the affected family, the hell away before disaster can strike. Joe Gill's comic script follows the film faithfully and Gill, who did much work for Charlton, does the best he can with the material. Despite a bit of help from Vince Colletta's inking, John Tartaglione's pencils are uninspired. A scene when the heroine is attacked by a killer plant is just as ludicrous in the comic as it is in the movie.

In 1966 Gold Key issued an adaptation of the wonderfully absurd *Fantastic Voyage*, in which a team in a sub is shrunk to microscopic size and injected into an artery of an important scientist whose brain

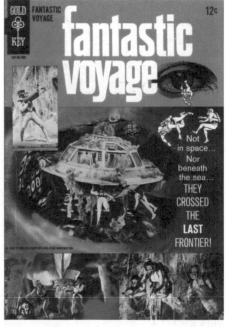

turned in a better-than-usual art job. The characters all look exactly like the actors — including Lloyd Bridges, David McCallum and Brian Kelly — who portrayed them in the movie.

In 1968, 35 years after its initial release in 1933, Gold Key came out with a giant 64-page adaptation of the classic *King Kong*. Beautifully done, the comic was almost as exciting, suspenseful, and entertaining as the movie. There were some minor changes made from the film. The characters, especially Ann Darrow and Carl Denham, look nothing like the actors who portrayed them. The comic, scripted by Gary Poole, eliminates the more gruesome scenes of the movie (which were excised after the film's initial release) depicting Kong chewing on people, stomping on natives, and throwing a poor woman out of her hotel room. The scene with Kong attacking and bashing the elevated subway is also not depicted. The comic adds a scene when Kong battles two horned Triceratops, and expands on the sequence when Ann and Jack Driscoll escape from the big ape by fleeing down the river. In one scary panel Kong's giant hand reaches into the water and nearly grabs the couple as they swim away underwater. Another change has the

ape battling the big snake not in Kong's lair as in the movie but at the foot of the mountain instead.

The art by Giovanni Ticci and Alberto Giolitti is generally first-rate, especially good in the scenes depicting a reptile rising from a river to overturn a raft upon which Denham, Driscoll and their fellow crew members are attempting to reach the other side. Other knock-out panels show Kong bursting through the wall built by the natives, escaping his chains in the Broadway theater, and trying to swat away the planes as they fly at him near the Empire State Building. Oddly, the characters are depicted with 1960's-style hair cuts and clothing, but the climax still uses the old-fashioned bi-planes of the movie. The first appearance of Kong in the comic is not nearly as dramatic as in the picture. Otherwise, this is arguably the best of the fantastic movie adaptations. George Wilson's cover painting is outstanding.

The Valley of Gwangi, which came out in 1969, was a major dinosaur flick with superb stop motion effects by Ray Harryhausen. A circus hopes to attract new business with a little prehistoric horse that escaped from a hidden valley, but the circus gets more than it bargained for when it captures a full-grown Tyrannosaurus rex that escapes from its cage a la King Kong and rampages in the village. The uncredited script of the Dell comic follows the movie fairly closely but it nearly eliminates the climax, the very best thing in the movie, when the T-Rex pads around inside a gigantic Cathedral as the hero tries to evade and/or destroy it. Artist Jack Sparling did not offer up an especially notable art job, although there is a fairly impressive full-size panel of the first dramatic appearance of the T-Rex, known as Gwangi, and some of the dino-action is reasonably well-done. The hero in the comic does resemble actor James Franciscus. The front cover boasts the beautiful painting for the movie's poster, which was drawn by Frank McCarthy.

Gold Key issued a comic book tie-in with *Beneath the Planet of the Apes* in 1970. This terrible sequel to the extremely popular *Planet of the Apes* had earth astronauts from the past involved with unpleasant talking apes and mutated humans with mental powers who worship a hydrogen bomb. In both movie and comic the earth is blown apart at the end. The uncredited

script follows the movie very closely, and the art by Alberto Giolitti and Sergio Costa is more than acceptable if not first-rate. Oddly, the lead characters greatly resemble the actors Charlton Heston and James Franciscus but only in a couple of panels.

It should be noted that if you're looking for really fine comic book versions of classic sci fi novels, you can do no better than the Classics Illustrated entries for **The Time Machine** and **Journey to the Center of the Earth**, among others. There were a few other fantastic movie adaptations that I have not yet come across: *The Magic Sword; X, The Man with X-Ray Eyes; War-Gods of the Deep; Darby O'Gill and the Little People*. The Dell comic version of *Forbidden Planet* isn't even available on ebay as of this writing, although I would imagine it is a prized collectible. Maybe someday I'll get my hands on it!

• • •

JAMES McKIMMEY'S LONG RUN
The Dell First Editions
by J. Charles Burwell

One of the pleasures of paperback collecting and reading is the discovery of a writer who has created compelling and original stories but who has not received the recognition afforded his or her contemporaries. Most knowledgeable fans of mid-century crime fiction can rattle off the works they've read by John D. MacDonald, David Goodis, and Jim Thompson. Dig a little deeper and they may have delved into ace scribes like Harry Whittington, Gil Brewer, Charles Williams, and the ubiquitous Day Keene. Thanks to the commiserating of collectors and dealers at the early pulp and paperback shows, the word got out about these crime fiction stalwarts and their notoriety grew with the advent of internet communication. Many of their novels began reappearing in bookstores thanks to the Black Lizard line of paperbacks in the 1980s and, somewhat later, the initial run of Hard Case Crime. It became, and continues to be, important to read their stories in order to get a complete picture of American Noir and some of its more indispensable manifestations.

But couched within this tradition are some fine writers who were undeservedly more obscure but ripe for rediscovery by fans of good hardboiled fiction. Such is the case with James McKimmey, who only recently has begun to receive the attention his well-crafted and dynamic novels deserve. For this writer, I first heard of McKimmey through an article the late Bill Crider wrote about Dell First Editions, a strong line of paperback originals that rivaled Gold Medal books for compulsively quick reads in the Crime and Western genres. In his "Dell First Editions," anthologized in **The Big Book of Noir** (Carroll and Graf, 1998), Crider provides a short history of the imprint and then cites a group of its key suspense writers, along with comments about their work and recommended novels to read. Among them is McKimmey. Crider compares him to John D. MacDonald and cites his ability to write "taut stories about ordinary people caught up in extraordinary circumstances . . . You can hardly go wrong by picking up any of his books, but try not to miss **Squeeze Play** and **The Long Ride**." Well, that was enough for this avid collector and reader to hear, so I immediately began seeking out copies of these two works. I soon discovered that McKimmey had penned a whole run of novels for the Dell FE line, seven in all between 1957 and 1962, well within the mid-century "Hardboiled Era." To further whet my appetite, one of these paperback originals featured a blurb on the back cover from John D. himself: "This man can manipulate tension and character in ways that are beginning to alarm me." I wondered, just what was MacDonald talking about?

Is he alarmed by the presence of a gifted competitor? Or is he expressing his own appreciation for the stories that McKimmey was creating and unfolding? Truth be told, McKimmey himself acknowledged John D.'s influence and his work has a similar flavor in terms of their range of characters and the tumultuous events that befall them. But McKimmey was writing about human beings and their struggles and clearly puts his own stamp on their interactions and the world they take place in.

In his notes on McKimmey, Bill Crider points out that the writer mysteriously disappeared from the paperback racks. His bibliography indicates that his last piece of crime fiction came out in 1972 and that he wrote some pieces for the juvenile market in the late '70s and early '80s. His run of seven novels for Dell all rolled out in a compressed five year period and they can be viewed as a kind of creative cycle. He produced some additional crime novels in the '60s, but not at such a prolific pace. This distinct burst of creative output is one of the intriguing things about McKimmey, and is the focus of this article.

James McKimmey was born in Holdredge, Nebraska in 1923, lived in some small towns in that vast state, eventually moving to the city of Omaha at the age of 13. He initially attended the University of Nebraska, but his education was interrupted (as it was for many) by World War II. He served in Europe with the 102nd Infantry Division. After the war and with separation from the armed forces, he returned to college, only this time at the University of San Francisco. He had already made the decision to be a professional writer, and began writing for the college newspaper as well as some local publications. Like many writers who eventually transitioned to paperback originals, he apprenticed by penning stories for the pulps, within the science fiction, western, and adventure genres. He was able to move on to the better-paying slicks, and, notably, published a story in a 1957 issue of *Cosmopolitan*, "Riot at Willow Creek," which later was expanded into his initial Dell First Edition, **The Perfect Victim** (1957).

The Perfect Victim takes place in what proves to be one of McKimmey's customary settings: a small farming community situated somewhere in the American midwest. It's a seemingly peaceful place with a population of only 1500. Everyone knows just about everybody here and their world is strictly a local one of warm diners, quiet pool halls, neat homes with well-manicured lawns, and unobtrusive hotels with clean, furnished rooms. The people who don't work in town work on the surrounding farms or the grain elevator that serves them. George Cary, who runs the community's newspaper, has unrealized journalistic ambitions, but instead has settled for the quiet life, with little else to report but the weather and agricultural news.

As the novel progresses, the quiet little town, named Willow Creek, is revealed to be a stultifying bastion of conformity, one with inflexible expectations of behavior and little tolerance for anyone who deviates from the middle American norm. Because of the town's small size, the residents have a painfully close view of everyone's business, and any stranger is immediately viewed with suspicion. Their big hang-up is, of course, sex, and crossing the town's repressive standards becomes a cause for deceit, manipulation, and uncontrolled violence.

Into this insulated world steps one Al Jackson, a traveling farm equipment salesman, based in Omaha, who roams his territory earning his commissions and padding his expense account. It's revealed that he has a wife and son at home, but takes his opportunities for on-the-road dalliances when he can get them. Like many salesmen, he's a glad-hander, quick with the jokes and quips, and fond of good whiskey and cheap cigars. Once he blows into the town of Willow Creek, he quickly goes to the local diner for a stack of wheats and coffee, and to size up his prospects.

One of those prospects is the waitress, Grace Amons, a voluptuous redhead who all the customers flirt with to one degree or another. Al Jackson doesn't hesitate to join in, immediately baiting her with compliments and not so veiled innuendo.

And he does this loudly, while trying to engage the diner's other customers at the same time. None of this goes over well, and the townies begin to take a quick dislike to him. Only *they* are allowed to flirt with Grace (or, as it turns out, go even further), and certainly not some Johnny Come Lately stranger who doesn't even live there.

All of this is witnessed by two youngsters sipping soda pop in the corner: Roger Cook, son of the local banker, and his college fraternity brother, Buggie Alstair, who is visiting him for the summer. Roger is presented as an innocent soul, whereas the older Buggie appears more wise to the ways of the world, being from Hollywood of all places. Like any healthy college boys, they are lusting after Grace too, and think a lot about what they can do about it. Their plans will ultimately precipitate the conflict and violence that eventually engulf Willow Creek.

Grace, who is a natural but well-meaning voluptuary, is secretly in a bind; she is two months pregnant. Although she has been having an affair with the local sheriff's teenage son, Chuck Beaman, she isn't quite sure that he is the father. Only the local country doctor, Old Doc Granger, knows of her condition, and she is racking her brain about what to do. Given the year that the novel came out (1957), it was well before Roe vs. Wade, so ending her pregnancy is not even mentioned in the narration. Grace is going to have her baby, the question for her is how to support it and still live her life. She begins to think seriously about this, which is not a frequent or customary activity for her. At this point in the tale, the college boys' lust and Grace's hasty need to be an "honest woman" come

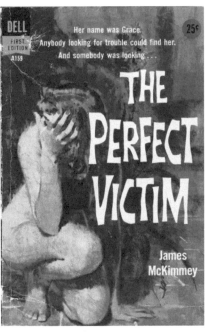

together with tragic consequences. She agrees to have a date with them in her room at the local hotel and asks them to bring a bottle along to spark the party. Before they climb the long stairway to her floor with great expectations, they have a long discussion about who will get to her first. Will it be Roger, who is painfully shy and sensitive? Or will it be the older and more experienced Buggie, dominant in his role as the other boy's fraternity brother and generally able to lead and manipulate him. It's clear to both of them that Buggie will take the lead in this situation.

But Grace has other ideas. She is somewhat put off by the older boy's aggressiveness and frankly sees Roger as someone more easily controlled. Besides, she calculates, he's a good boy from a good family and he surely will marry her if she can seduce him and tie that in with her already unfolding pregnancy. The alcohol is quickly imbibed and one thing leads to another. Grace makes the most of her opportunity with Roger in another room, all while Buggie seethes, his rage growing by the minute.

After losing his virginity, Roger briefly returns to his friend who high-handedly convinces him to leave, leaving him alone to take his "turn" with the sexy redhead. This is an almost painful scene to read, with Roger's first sexual experience cheapened by Buggie's dominance and by Grace's obvious disappointment with his hasty exit, so soon after their warm coupling. Moreover, she's in no mood to quickly turn around and satisfy Buggie, so she asks him to leave too. Buggie isn't having it; he forces himself on Grace, cursing in her ear, and they scuffle, noisily and roughly.

He viciously shoves her into the wall and her head strikes a hard wooden bureau. She slumps and falls to the floor, dead, her half-open eyes peering vacantly into space. Roger, who has returned to the apartment (after being spooked by the sight of people out on the street), stares down at her in frightened disbelief.

With cold-blooded assurance, Buggie convinces Roger that they can avoid responsibility (and prison) and simply sneak away from the scene without implicating themselves. They do so quietly, and, as they leave the hotel, who should come in but the outsider, Al Jackson, drunk as a skunk and clumsily trying to light a cigar. After greeting the boys incoherently, he too heads up the stairs to Grace's room, hoping for his own blissful tryst. He goes in, and, in his inebriated state, doesn't see the corpus delicti, and assumes it's not his night. However, he leaves behind a tell-tale clue: his half-smoked cigar, like Grace, cold and lifeless on the floor.

It is this one piece of circumstantial evidence that lands Jackson in the local jail, virtually confirming the suspicions the citizens of Willow Creek already harbor against him. What follows in the balance of the novel is an indictment of the town's small-mindedness and its easily evoked desire for violent revenge. Ultimately, a frightening lynch-mob mentality is revealed, along with a ready willingness to administer justice based on emotions rather than real facts and evidence. Citing again the date of this story — 1957 — it takes place well within the American era of extra-legal executions without benefit of trial.

McKimmey peppers this compelling plot with vivid characterizations: Sheriff Beaman, who chooses to railroad Jackson without clear evidence, Roger's father, another failed authority figure, who, after learning the truth, hasn't the courage to stand up for his son, and George Cary, who risks everything to find that truth along with his soul. And there is Roger, frightened and uncertain, who reaches a crossroads in his journey from boy to man. Will he break away from Buggie's dominance? Will he take the safe way out or will he overcome his guilt and do the right thing?

Finally, there is Buggie, the master manipulator, who calculatingly manufactures innuendo and outright lies, stirring the simple townsfolk to a homicidal frenzy. All while getting off on the process. It becomes clear that this is what stimulates and excites him, more than sex or booze. Two of his interactions with "adults" reveal his true motivations:

Shortly after Grace's death, the two boys return to Roger's home and share some wine with his staid middle-class parents. Roger's father, the town banker, opines about the small-town values of Willow Creek. He talks about the importance of proper conduct and how tradition comes from the "undistinguished" multitudes, "who are a contributing part of society" as opposed to "any special single opposer of tradition who views from the outside . . . A reaction against tradition usually comes from a single opposer. To defy tradition, you usually have to do it alone. One man against the world." To this homily, Buggie responds, "Well, isn't that how progress is made? . . . Isn't it always that one violator who points the way, who starts out what might eventually become tradition?" Roger's father, acting as if the conversation is a polite intellectual exercise, points out that the traditions of the multitudes stand the test of time, whereas the lone opposer's opinion "may be nothing more than a whim — sometimes a madman's whim at that." Without realizing it, the senior Cook has evoked Buggie's true motivation, to shake things up and be "that one violator."

Later on in the novel, Buggie blatantly tells newspaperman Cary about his manipulations and how he has twisted Willow Creek to the brink of self-destruction. Without the tiniest shred of remorse, he is quite open about his efforts, all while knowing Cary is in the minority and can do nothing to save Al Jackson or the town itself. Cary admits that the town has "a problem" and Buggie responds with an explanation about what makes him tick:

"The problem is stupidity, isn't it? I've got no stake in anybody here. I really don't give a damn, sir, whether or not Willow Creek dries

up and blows off the map. So I can see what you've got here. And so it's like standing on a hill and watching two trains meeting each other on the same track. You know there's going to be a collision, and yet it doesn't matter because you're not on either one of those trains . . . I'm far enough down the hill to have access to the switches, too. What I mean, I can make damn sure the trains are on the right track . . . I wonder, sir, . . . how it would impress you if I were to say I've been pulling certain switches in Willow Creek?"

Buggie goes on to reveal everything to Cary, who doesn't want to believe what he is hearing. It's a chilling scene, for Cary and the reader, and a unique portrait of evil. And **The Perfect Victim** is a unique portrait of a small town transformed by lies, rage, and its own foolish intolerance.

In his next Dell First Edition, McKimmey shifts into the first-person mode of fiction, and the result is a hardboiled classic, firmly in that American tradition. **Winner Take All** (1959) leaves the small-town environment and takes place in the noir triangle of San Francisco, Reno, and Los Angeles. Its protagonist is Mark Steele, ostensibly an engineer, but really a drifter, a soldier of fortune and tough guy, looking for love and money, and taking them whenever and wherever he can. He tells his story in a wry self-deprecating monologue, the reader always knowing what he's thinking, whether he's drinking alone, or dealing directly with thugs or beautiful women. He's able to find humor in the most serious of circumstances. McKimmey demonstrates a mastery of this style throughout the novel; it has the flavor of a film noir voice-over. You can almost hear Robert Mitchum or Dick Powell recounting this tale over a pack of Camels and a bottle of Old Forester.

The novel's beginning finds Steele newly arrived in a seedy San Fran hotel, waiting for something to happen and wondering what to do next. He doesn't have to wait long, he's soon visited by one Thomas Byrd, a rich ne'er do well who claims to be his long-lost twin brother. Separated at birth, Byrd has lived in the lap of luxury without having to work, while Steele has had to scrap for a living from one place to another. Seeing that they do look alike, the initially suspicious Steele doesn't take too long to believe the man's story (and, of course, neither does the reader) and soon wants to know why Byrd has looked him up. Byrd tells him he has a simple proposition: he wants Steele to pose as him in order to settle a huge gambling debt he has incurred in Reno. He's in dutch with a dangerous gambler named Nicole to the tune of 100 Gs. Even with his obvious wealth, Byrd claims that's too much for him to pay at once. Moreover, his gambling habit has gotten him into trouble before, he doesn't want his rich uncle or wife to know the extent of the fix he's in. His solution is to send in Byrd to negotiate a lowering of the debt, or at least a series of payments that he can manage. Having Steele as his "tin mitten" will allow him the freedom to handle the financial piece. For his trouble, Byrd has promised to pay Steele 10 grand, provided he's successful in closing a deal.

Steele remains suspicious of Byrd and suspicious of the whole scenario. But, given his strapped circumstances, 10 Gs is 10 Gs and nothing to sneeze at. So he agrees to join in on the ruse and the novel's action shifts to the gambling world of Reno, Nevada. Posing as Byrd, Steele has a series of encounters with Nicole's hired thugs and also with two women, both of them beautiful and both very different.

In a fly-by-night hotel casino, he quickly establishes his new persona as the high stakes gambler Thomas Byrd, and he also meets a voluptuous brunette named Linda. After some flirtatious repartee, they repair to his room for an urgent tryst. Before they can do anything, he spies someone watching them from the balcony. Linda does not see the intruder and Steele, showing his true colors as a man, sends her away, presumably to safety. She sees this as a rude brush-off and walks away angry. It looks like it's over between them but she remains an important although not prominent figure in the novel.

Following her exit, Steele confronts the furtive figure on the balcony and easily overcomes him in a fist fight. It's the casino croupier, sent by Nick Nicole to ferret out Byrd and collect on his debt. He wants the entire 100G wad and Steele (as Byrd) isn't having it, he wants to deal with the man himself and be in a position to negotiate the number down. As Nicole's errand boy, the erstwhile peeping Tom can't believe this and tells Steele that if he doesn't pony up the cash, his life won't be worth a lead nickel.

The croupier is only the first of the emissaries sent by Nicole. Having seemingly lost out on Linda, Steele is only too willing to respond to the overtures of a beautiful blonde who comes on to him in the casino. They go out on a romantic car-ride into the surrounding country and make what seems to be a promising stop near an abandoned barn. Steele wastes no time getting into a clinch with the blonde doll when he is unceremoniously slugged from behind and knocked out. This has happened to a million private eyes in the naked city and McKimmey has some fun referencing that in Steele's ongoing monologue:

DELL
FIRST
EDITION
A185

25¢

Reno: The games are legit, it's the women you've got to watch — especially one named Linda

WINNER TAKE ALL

JAMES Mc KIMMEY

"It struck right in the middle of a kiss, and for a foolish instant I thought it was the power of Julie's charms-because something was exploding inside my head like the incandescence of an atomic bomb. For that same foolish moment, I sighed at the reaction this kid could get out of a man. But I knew as I started falling into that deep pool of blackness I'd always read about in the detective books, that it wasn't Julie who sent me there, but a hard and well-aimed blow squarely against the back of my head."

When Steele comes to, he is confronted with two more of Nicole's thugs, incongruously named Freddie and Billy. They cuff him around some but, in his role as Byrd, he convinces them to accept a check for $50,000 and deliver it to Nicole. End of story, right? Not by a long shot. Steele gets rid of Julie, returns to his hotel, makes up to Linda, arranges to meet with her in his room, and summarily gets knocked out <u>again</u>.

He wakes up, and Freddie and Billy are back, this time with a gun. They let him know that the check has bounced, there's not a cent in Byrd's bank account, and it's the end of the line. Steele punches out the light and McKimmey treats the reader to a knock down, drag out fight, completely conducted in the dark. This is a dynamic scene, and Steele emerges on top this time, knocking out Freddie but not before he has inadvertently shot his partner in the leg.

Clearly a man of endurance, Steele leaves the plug-uglies to their own devices, packs his bag, and gets ready to return to Frisco. With the knowledge of the bounced check, he realizes that Byrd has played him for a sucker. In fact, Byrd has now virtually disappeared, having previously been in touch with Steele during every step of their ruse. So, now Steele has to shift gears. Not only does he have to find Byrd and square accounts, he also has to stay out of the reach of Nicole and his minions, who continue to think he's really Byrd. So far, the only good thing to come out of the mess is his relationship with the beautiful Linda. Steele has come clean with her, telling her the whole story, and he is amazed to find that she still wants to be with him. And the feeling is mutual and growing. Within the trappings of his rough and tumble persona, Steele is beginning to emerge as a right guy, able to really care for someone and willing to do the right thing.

The balance of this fast-moving novel involves Steele's pursuit of Byrd from San Francisco to Los Angeles. Along the way, he encounters another one of Nicole's emissaries (a mild-looking but coldly sadistic hit man in a Homburg hat), a murder is committed, and there is a final confrontation with Byrd in a lonely beachside cottage. Nick Nicole, who has been remote and offstage for nearly the entirety of the story, makes a late and threatening appearance at its denouement.

In **Winner Take All**, McKimmey has crafted a satisfying and action-packed tale that is just plain fun to read. Steele is a likable protagonist, admirable in his dogged persistence to right wrongs and get his due rewards. And while he's clearly a good guy, he's not so good that he won't throw his fists around or try a little deception to get where he needs to be. It is tempting to this reader to think that Steele could have been a fine figure for an ongoing series in the Shell Scott or Brad Dolan mode, but it appears that McKimmey never revisited the character. And, in his Dell First Edition cycle, he never again exercised his chops with a first-person narrative. In the next installment, he would return to his third-person style, as well as to a small-town setting, with its conflict and deadly consequences.

Cornered!, published as a Dell First Edition in 1960, takes place in Arrow Junction, another small farm community, this time located in California. But it's similar to **Perfect Victim's** Willow Creek; it's a provincial setting, everyone knows everybody's business, and the citizens are divided between those who are naturally friendly and those who have small-town hang-ups. (Or worse.) But for an outsider, it might appear to be a perfect place to hide out. Or to find someone who wants to.

The novel opens a short distance from town at a roadside filling station. It's cold and a snowstorm is well on its way. A sedan rolls in for a fill-up, driven by two professional hit-men, Billy (again?) and Al. It is revealed that they are looking for a beautiful blonde named Annie. Unfortunately for her, she stumbled onto the scene of a murder committed by Billy's brother, Tony. She ended up being the prosecution's star witness in Tony's trial and he is sitting on Death Row in San Quentin, only days before his last exit in the gas chamber. His only reason for living is to be sure that Annie dies before he does. To this end, he has enlisted his brother to terminate her breathing before his own is silenced by California cyanide. He has promised his brother a cool 50 grand if he can do the job on schedule.

Although he's a professional, it turns out that Billy has an itchy trigger finger. His and Al's exit from the gas station is delayed by their need to get tire-chains for the oncoming storm. The station's owner, Corly, is a bit too sociable and this adds to Billy's impatience. Things quickly go awry when a local truck driver shows up followed by the sheriff. Corly is yakking away with them, says the word "sheriff" and Billy is convinced they've been made. He brings his gun out and starts firing. So does the sheriff and so does partner Al. When the smoke clears, Al, Corly, and the lawman are lying dead in the falling snow and the truck driver is trembling underneath his farm rig.

As badly as things have turned out, Billy is unfazed, even though he's wounded in the arm. He's going to finish this job and grab those 50Gs. But his car is up on the garage's lift and he has no way to get it down. Certainly not wanting to hang around with this tableau, Billy high-tails it out of there and heads for the nearby train yards.

McKimmey moves the action to Arrow Junction itself, and the scene is the local cafe, not unlike the one in **Perfect Victim's** Willow Creek. Only this time, the focus is on its owner, Bob Saywell, and not on a sexy waitress. McKimmey presents Saywell as some kind of unofficial mayor of Willow Creek. He's nosy, wants to know everyone's business, and looks to maintain a hugely influential role in the community, getting whatever he can in the process. And he's got his eyes on a beautiful outsider, Ann Burley, who's recently moved to town, having entered into a hasty and ill-considered marriage to a local farmer.

Like Buggie in **The Perfect Victim**, Saywell is an ace manipulator and he knows how to get information and use it to his advantage. Through a perusal of the newspapers and his own network of contacts, Saywell figures out that Mrs. Burley really is homicide witness Annie and that she is hiding from something. Why else would she change the color of her hair and marry a local boy so quickly? Moreover, while in his cafe, Ann hears the news about the gas station killings and promptly faints. Saywell can tell she's scared and virtually alone in her attempted anonymity. With deliberate calculation, he begins concocting a plan to get her under his thumb and into his bed.

After she panics and drops to the floor in Saywell's cafe, she is helped by the local town physician, who treats her and then gives her a ride home. Hugh Stewart is a failed surgeon from back east, who also has recently moved to Arrow Junction and established himself as a simple country doctor. McKimmey paints him as another outsider; like Ann, he is hiding from something, but it's his past and not an actual threat of death. He is a young and good-looking man and there is an undeniable spark between him and Ann that they are hardly aware of. But Saywell is aware of it, and their growing attraction for each other quickly becomes part of his plan. Besides, Stewart's outsider status irks Saywell and he would like nothing better than to bring the young physician down a notch.

But first he tries to get to Ann. Saywell confronts her at home, revealing what he knows about her true identity and

DELL
FIRST EDITION
8197

35¢

She couldn't run any more from the two men who wanted her— both for different reasons

CORNERED!

James McKimmey

threatening to tell all to the good citizens of Arrow Junction. Of course, there's a way she can avoid this and preserve her cover, she simply has to be "nice" to Saywell whenever he wants her to be. This proposition scares Ann but angers her even more and she pointedly refuses to submit to this revolting man. Undeterred, Saywell takes another step towards stirring things up and goes to her husband, Ted Burley.

With farmer Burley, McKimmey creates a small sub-plot in the novel that reveals character and adds another layer to its events. For all his standing in the community, Burley is a twisted personality and his marriage to the beautiful Ann is a troubled one. Put simply, he's a mama's boy, he hasn't grown up, and he remains in his parents' thrall long after their passing. Moreover, he is deeply conflicted about sex and his reaction to Ann's wifely overtures is not passion but a seething anger and revulsion. Tellingly, they sleep in separate rooms and beds, his being the same cot he's been in since childhood.

So Burley becomes even more twisted when Saywell goes to him and intimates that Ann is having an affair with young Dr. Stewart. Irate and unreasonable, he confronts her with the story and refuses to believe her emphatic denials. This drives her out of the house and back to town, not only having to hide from Saywell and would-be assassin Billy, but also her own husband. Ironically enough, she again seeks assistance from Hugh Stewart.

The remaining chapters of **Cornered!** bring together a number of other Arrow Junction figures and places them all in Saywell's cafe, where they are held hostage by hit man Billy. Time is ticking away towards his brother's execution and he is anxious to complete his job, collect his money, and escape to what he views as the "promised land" of South America.

The scenes in the cafe are slowly played out with the stress and danger posed by Billy, building on itself, minute by minute and hour by hour. Besides his criminal intent, he is revealed to possess a sadistic streak, intimidating each hostage with threats, bullying, and humiliation. He easily cows the usually controlling Saywell into calling all over for Ann while, at the same time, serving the hostages breakfast and coffee. Aroused by a female hostage's beauty, he blatantly propositions her in front of her husband, all while waving his gun and daring him to do something about it. He arrogantly forces the doctor to fix his arm while pointing a gun at his head.

Meanwhile, the local police have learned of the situation and, led by Sheriff Jenkins, they are outside the cafe, surrounding it with guns drawn. Jenkins clearly is a small-town cop, and he is scared, unsure if he can rise to this kind of occasion.

Ultimately, the entire tableau comes down to a question of who will act and how. McKimmey deftly brings in twin themes of failure and redemption; where how the characters respond to Billy and Ann determines who dies and who survives. And, for those who do survive, whether their self-respect will remain, battered and scarred but nevertheless intact. With his skillful interweaving of the characters' motivations and fates, he has created another compelling tale of small-town drama and conflict. **Cornered!** delivers the goods, page after page.

McKimmey's next two installments in his Dell cycle can be seen as companion pieces. **24 Hours To Kill** and **The Wrong Ones**, both published in 1961 have, at their core, the world of the Juvenile Delinquent. With the advent of films like *West Side Story* and *Rebel Without A Cause* as well as paperback novels with titles like **The Blackboard Jungle**, **Tomboy**, and **Zip-Gun Angels**, a newsworthy youth crime wave took on a prominent role in popular culture during the 1950s and early '60s.

The sordid and violent activities of gangs in America's cities were depicted with a romantic energy and verve that was both dramatic and shocking. These seemingly realistic tales of juvenile crime drew people to movie theaters or the paperback spinner racks and made compelling figures out of black-jacketed thugs with DA haircuts, switchblades, and long rap sheets. Equally compelling were their women; teenage girls actually, but ripened enough to dip their toes (among other things) in the swirling waters of risk and desire.

Given the times, it made sense for McKimmey to jump on the JD bandwagon and he does so with some of his customary settings and establishment citizens, but he also introduces a range of characters that incorporate both the appeal and the danger associated with this new kind of criminal. With their heightened profile in the public consciousness, McKimmey focuses his writer's eye on how the community responds to them; with terror, desire, or the need to exploit and control.

In **24 Hours To Kill**, McKimmey again returns to his favorite setting, the small town that is both insular and isolated. Blue Valley is situated in Western Colorado near a great powerful river. Like the blizzard that spurs much of the action in **Cornered!**, the land surrounding Blue Valley is besieged by a raging rainstorm. The river is beginning to rise and the roads into town are starting to flood. Most of the town's citizens are already engaged in building a wall of sandbags, an effort to restrain, even by inches, the seemingly unstoppable deluge.

In the middle of this severe weather crisis, a sheriff and his deputy are transporting a vicious young criminal to face trial for multiple homicides. Jack Kelty looks like a clean-cut college boy; blonde, handsome and neatly dressed. But he already has several alleged murders to his credit and has also shot a police officer, severely wounding him. Given that it's 1961, he surely will be facing execution once he's presented to judge and jury. When he complains about his treatment by law enforcement, citing his rights as a citizen, the deputy he's handcuffed to poses the question, "When did dead men have rights?"

But, because of his youth and good-looks, as well as his supposedly humble beginnings, Kelty has his champions too. Chief among them is Martin Hillary, a popular columnist for a widely-circulated newspaper. In contrast to George Cary of **The Perfect Victim,** a small-town newspaperman who recaptures his journalistic idealism, Hillary is a perfect cynic, wanting only to shape the public mood and build his paper's circulation. He does this by painting Kelty as a victim of both a deprived upbringing and a malevolent police force. Relentlessly pursuing this story, and looking to sensationalize it even further, he sticks close to this miscreant, rankling the police while also attracting an entourage of five borderline delinquents. This motley crew of teenagers features a leader who drives a low-riding Mercury and carries a gun, and his *segundo*, a knife specialist known only as "Cut." The rest of the gang of teenagers includes a shameless womanizer, a huge plug-ugly who likes to break things (and people), and a masochistic jester who serves as the butt of the others' jokes. Nodding acquaintances of the somewhat older Kelty, they regard him as some kind of inspiration. Reading Martin's column and following his trail, they have developed a half-baked plan to rescue their hero from the clutches of the law. As ludicrous as this might seem, their plan eventually has a serious impact on Kelty, the police, and the citizens of Blue Valley.

Throughout his novels' depictions of small-town life, McKimmey has frequently brought in the figure of the "outsider," someone who, uninvited, disrupts the

DELL

FIRST EDITION

B169

35¢

24 HOURS TO KILL

Sometimes death wears the face of a trigger-happy punk —or a young girl with ideas too bad for her own good.

By James McKimmey

fabric of the community and tests its assumptions about life and morality. Such a figure may do this inadvertently or with malevolent purpose. There is Al Jackson, the hapless salesman in **The Perfect Victim** or Billy, the sadistic hit-man in **Cornered!** In **24 Hours To Kill**, there, is, obviously, Kelty, Martin, and the gang. But McKimmey also introduces a different kind of outsider, someone who lives in Blue Valley, but is not fully accepted by the people who live there. This is Deputy Sheriff Steve Michaels, who grew up in the town as a kid from the proverbial "wrong side of the tracks," was actually sent away to reform school, and returned to the community as an ostensibly responsible adult. As a teacher, sports coach, and now the local law, he has become a respected young man. He's gotten close to the town's Mayor, Ben Blake, and even has become engaged to his beautiful and sensible older daughter, Sue. At the outset of the novel, he is presented as someone who truly has steered his life in the right direction. It's pointed out that, with other choices, he could have become another Jack Kelty.

But in a provincial community like Blue Valley, his past is not so easily shaken off. There are those who remember Steve's early life and wonder if he's really changed. They remain suspicious of his character and, as the events of the novel unfold, resist his suddenly assumed authority.

The pivotal event that precipitates the story's conflicts is the collapse of a dam caused by the storm's swelling of the river just outside of Blue Valley. This releases a torrent of water just as the two lawmen are driving with Kelty across a local bridge. Their car is washed off the bridge, drowning the sheriff instantly and imperiling Kelty and the deputy, who are handcuffed to each other. Almost miraculously, they are rescued by a local farmer, who assumes they're both criminals. He forcibly delivers them to the Blue Valley jail at gunpoint, where they are properly identified. Kelty is placed in a cell while the deputy tries to recover from his brush with a watery death. Anticipating that the storm would cause such a detour, Hillary Martin is already there, waiting with his typewriter and ready to wring whatever drama he can from an already tense set of circumstances. Knowing this, the Mercury full of delinquents has followed him to Blue Valley and they are now camping out in a local pool parlor, plotting their next move.

The dam-burst and ensuing flood have cut off all access to the town, making it a virtual island and even more isolated than before. Moreover, most of its citizens are on the other side of the river, trying in vain to hold back the water with a wall of sandbags and their own sweat and gristle. Left behind in Blue Valley are Steve Michaels, along with Mayor Blake, his few cronies and his family. McKimmey throws two wild cards into this situation One of them is Gretchen, Blake's younger daughter. A teenager with the ripe body of a woman, she operates in the story as an uncontrolled loose cannon, willfully disappearing under the eyes of her parents, stealing her sister's car, and insinuating herself into the jailhouse, all to get provocatively close to Kelty, the fascinating bad boy.

The other wild card is Emil Dorne, a leading Blue Valley denizen, whose true character is revealed as that of a gun-toting Ugly American. Another one of McKimmey's disturbing sadists, he is eagerly waiting for an armed confrontation, and, in this regard, the presence of Kelty and his JD fan-club is grist for the thick venom running through his veins. While not even a lawman himself, he is contemptuous of Steve, and sees himself in his mirror as a true bastion of law and order. He is an accident waiting to happen, and this has disastrous results.

All of these elements converge over the course of a dark night of the soul, where risks are taken, violence ensues, and limits are sorely tested. Steve Michaels, the outsider, must overcome real danger and protect a town that doesn't fully trust him, all the while wondering if he'll survive into the next morning. McKimmey lays the action on swiftly with some unexpected surprises, but without sacrificing any depth of character. By the end of **24 Hours To Kill**, Blue Valley is still standing but not everyone has survived. And those who have are irrevocably changed, for better or worse. And McKimmey's skill as a writer makes one care, page after page.

With **The Wrong Ones**, McKimmey's other Juvenile Delinquent novel, he takes an entirely different approach with the plot, while still incorporating the requisite JD milieu of gangs, guns, and sexually provocative teenagers. Simply put, he fashions a whodunit, starting the story with the discovery of a corpse, draped inside a Chevrolet convertible parked unobtrusively by the beach. The reader is told that the dead man is Allan Decker, a slickly handsome clinical psychologist from the local youth detention program. With multiple flashbacks and personality switches, a parade of intertwined characters are presented as all having a motive for desiring his conclusive demise. But this is no "Corpse at the Garden Party" classical mystery. The story is a skillful blend of the era's gang culture, the human service workers who deal with errant teenagers, and the police who want to put those miscreants away. To this mix, McKimmey adds some significant racial tension, and the lure of a sexy teenage girl who may or may not be a psychopath.

Much of the story's action is set in the youth detention center, an unusual setting for a crime thriller. And, while the cops naturally have a role in this murder mystery, there also is an overriding presence of human service workers; psychologist Decker, as well as two probation officers, Joe Burnett and Frank Upland. How these professionals do their jobs (and live their lives) is integral to the cause of the murder and the resulting suspicions cast on the delinquent youngsters going in and out of the center. Burnett is a compassionate workaholic, deeply concerned about the kids he serves and constantly worried about the path they will take in life. Not really naive, he nevertheless maintains a cockeyed optimism about their prospects. Upland is more circumspect and naturally suspicious. Like Burnett, he wants the best for their charges, but has lower expectations. The two POs are both trying to do right by their jobs and they frequently discuss the difficult choices they have to make. Their dialogues about the work is one of the more interesting aspects of the novel, highlighting a different angle on the nature of crime.

And then there is murder victim Allan Decker. In terms of integrity, he is quite the opposite of Burnett and Upland. He is revealed as an inveterate womanizer, coldly arrogant and manipulative. His list of female conquests doubles as the list of probable suspects in his killing: his beautiful and neglected wife, his married mistress, and even the spinsterish PBX operator at the detention center, who he teases and humiliates. But, most disturbingly, there is Wanda Mitchell.

Like Gretchen in **24 Hours To Kill**, Wanda is a strikingly sexy teenager on the cusp of womanhood. Fatherless, and sharing a studio apartment with her mother, she has been in and out of trouble, with several stints in the detention center to her credit. Part of her mandated supervision is "treatment" sessions with psychologist Decker. But, instead of anything therapeutic, he has harassed her relentlessly and it is quite clear that he has used his position to coerce her into having sex with him. And it's also clear that she resents it, and resents it deeply.

There are other men involved with these women and two of them line up as suspects. There is his mistress' rich and aging husband, who has one of the oldest motivations for murder. But more pivotal to the workings of the story is the figure of Mac Perkins, teenage gang leader and another sometime resident of the detention center.

Mac is the leader of The Black Leopards, a gang that, with the support of Burnett and Upland, are moving from violent rumbles to community service. This is not as far-fetched as it sounds, but what makes this club unusual is that it is composed of white working-class kids and Mac, their leader, is black (or, in the argot of the times, a "Negro"). McKimmey doesn't really explain how this came to happen, other than by portraying Mac as someone with natural leadership and a righteous intelligence. His influence over the Leopards is solid and rarely challenged. There is a telling scene early in the novel where the gang is meeting with a prospective member, Ducco, who rapidly displays his bigotry and utter disdain for Mac. Seeing this, the group wastes no time in voting him down and dismissing his application. Blindly enraged by this rejection, Ducco leaves, only to return with a switchblade after the meeting has broken up. Seeing Mac on the dark street alone, he abruptly attacks him with the knife and is soundly beaten for his efforts. Mac has shown that he is no stranger to street fighting and he sends Ducco off to crawl home, tears streaming down his face.

Mac indeed is tough but it turns out that Ducco might have gotten off easy. While he is alone in the clubhouse, it is revealed that Mac keeps a clean gun squirreled away in a cubbyhole. With this scene, McKimmey leaves it open as to whether Mac will make use of the weapon, either out of racial tension or for other reasons. And the beautiful Wanda Mitchell is one of those reasons. She baits the young black man relentlessly and their mutual sexual tension builds throughout the novel until it is tighter than a guitar string. She accepts him explicitly and he knows this, but, it is 1961, and he knows how dangerous it could be for him if he gives in to her advances. He becomes further unnerved when she tells him about the abuse she has suffered from Decker; this white man from the detention center can get away unscathed with such behavior while he could suffer greatly for touching the tempestuous Wanda. As strong and quiet as Mac appears to Burnett and Upland, he actually is deeply conflicted, and mostly about white people.

Written during a time that was well

within the Civil Rights movement, McKimmey provides some insight and commentary into the dynamics of its struggle. When Mac returns home after his encounter with Ducco, he speaks with his father and then his uncle, both of whom have contrasting views of established white society; his father advocating peaceful integration whereas his uncle is vehemently distrustful of any white person. The latter actually berates Mac for his interactions at the youth center and he really is influenced by both men. He is well aware of bigotry but he is young and trying to find his own way in life. Despite his inherent toughness, he is grappling with the choices he must make, not only in his community, but also with Wanda, and the trouble she could bring if he goes too far with her.

Later on in the novel, as the murder is investigated, Mac does find trouble and becomes a suspect, not just because of circumstantial evidence, but also due to his race. McKimmey presents the police as the dogged professionals that they are, but he also uncovers the bigots who can work in their midst. While probation officer Burnett commiserates with Inspector Majorki about the case, the latter tells him about the focus on Mac and points to a burly cop, Monk Maitland, who was sent to question him. Maitland admits that, in the process, he had to "rough him up a little" . . .

Majorki frowned. "I didn't get that report from you, Monk."

"Ah, you can't hurt them coons." Maitland laughed. "Heads like bowling balls, you know what I mean?" His smile faded for the first time, an ugliness swept over his face. "That

boy's been hanging around white boys too long-beginning to think he's one of them or something. I don't take that, see? I just don't take that off no boogy."

This naked exchange of bigotry enrages Burnett and he tells Majorki to keep his "gorilla" away from Mac and out of his jurisdiction. Threatening to bust Maitland's nose in the process, he storms out of the police station with Upland and they drive off. Upland tells Burnett to "take it easy." After a few minutes of weighty silence, Burnett is calm enough to speak his mind:

"I was just thinking, they ask teachers if they're communists before they let them teach. They ask soldiers if they like girls. They ask defense plant employees if they have police records. But they don't ask a sergeant on the police force if he's a racist before they turn him loose on a seventeen year old Negro. That's kind of funny, isn't it Frank?"

Upland responds by pointing out that Burnett gets all worked up because he thinks all these kids are "angels," even when the "fuse is lit." Burnett looks back at his friend and points out, "If I didn't, who would?"

Although seemingly dated on the surface (for 2021), McKimmey's 1961 depiction of good cops versus bigoted cops is striking and surprisingly contemporary. Moreover, the portrayal of the probation officers and their work adds a humanistic element to this whodunit, giving it a unique flavor. And, yet, **The Wrong Ones** is a solid piece of mid-century paperback crime fiction, created with the requisite grit, passion, and violence. It's a good read for fans of the juvenile delinquent sub-genre and, with the murder finally solved by the very last chapter, it's also a certifiable page-turner, suitable for long sleepless nights.

With **The Long Ride** (1961), (which some feel is the author's masterpiece), McKimmey steps away from his concerns with race and juvenile crime, and fashions a genuine road novel. He throws a disparate group of characters into one moving car, and forces them to confront one another with a range of emotions: passionate lust and greed, suspicion and deceit, genuine warmth and caring, and, with one protagonist, an unwavering desire for justice.

The tale begins with the prelude and execution of a bank robbery in the Midwest town of Loma City. Harry Wells, a recently discharged career Army sergeant, is parlaying that connection to steal a military payroll that is being held in the bank. His ruthless character is quickly exposed in the opening scene where he and his youthful partner, Willy Tyler, are holding a bank employee hostage. They have bound and tortured him for information, and later, with Tyler unknowingly waiting in their Plymouth, Wells disposes of him, quickly and quietly.

Posing as the employee and an ostensible job applicant, Tyler and Wells enter the bank, draw their guns, and grab a black satchel filled with Army cash. But things quickly go awry; alarms are set off and a gun battle ensues while they try to escape with the swag. The young Tyler, never really up for this kind of action, is shot badly, mortally wounded. In a final act of desperation, he flings the satchel across the garbage-strewn alley opposite the bank, and it falls, out of sight and hidden in the heat of the battle. Wells, frantically firing at the police and bank guards, realizes what Tyler has done but has no way to search and recover the satchel. He barely escapes arrest by jumping back into their getaway car and roaring off with the bullets flying.

All of this action has been observed through a window of the cheap tenement house next to the alley by Allan Garwith, a one-armed former athlete and petty criminal. Seeing the bloody Tyler fall to the

ground, Garwith races down the stairs and out to the alley, seemingly unconcerned about his own safety. With perfect timing, he steps outside just as Tyler tosses the loaded satchel, and, incredibly, it lands at his feet. Not needing to be told what it is, he grabs the bag and runs it up to his apartment, shoving it quickly under his bed.

It is this robbery, along with an almost casual comment made by Garwith's wife, Cicely, that sets up the events of the novel, all of which take place on a long road trip to San Francisco. Before his unexpected gift of the Army payroll, Garwith was at a dead end. Coming off a disastrous crime spree in New Orleans, where he lost his arm (and nearly his life), Garwith entered into a hasty marriage with a woman he really doesn't care for. He has no job or prospects, and Cicely, who has loved him since their childhood, does her best to lift his sagging spirits. She mentions their need to get a fresh start and she has learned of an opportunity to share a ride with a widowed matron, a Mrs. Landry, all the way to the West Coast. Initially unenthusiastic at this suggestion, Garwith now jumps at the chance to leave the scene of the crime and schemes to start another life with his newfound fortune but without his devoted wife.

Having presented the crime and the criminals, McKimmey then introduces the cast of characters who will all stuff themselves into Mrs. Landry's station wagon and embark on a sometimes dangerous and life-changing journey across the heart of the American West.

First is Wells himself. He has quickly ascertained the connection between Garwith and the missing boodle, also learning that he and his wife have signed up with Mrs. Landry's cross-country expedition. Advertising his Veteran status, and with stern military bearing, he is able to present himself as a suitable passenger and he is readily accepted into the group.

John Benson, posing as an executive of a small advertising firm, is really an FBI agent, leaving four years of desk work to go back into the dangers of field duty. In a conference with another agent, it is revealed that the Bureau already suspects

Wells for the payroll robbery; he worked in the Army finance detachment just prior to his discharge. Because he is unknown in Loma City, Benson is the perfect operative to travel undercover and observe Wells' actions first-hand. As the road trip begins, he realizes that Wells is paying close attention to Garwith and begins to wonder if they are working together. He needs to keep an eye on both of them, and this becomes a challenge, not just because of the suspects' natural shiftiness, but also due to the distractions provided by the remaining passengers in the wagon, all of them female.

Mrs. Landry, the trip's organizer and main driver, is a generous soul, good-hearted to a fault. She likes most people and, in her mind, will do her best to keep each member of the group happy and enthused. Having no real idea about what Wells, Benson, and Garwith are up to, she nonetheless can sense that something is amiss with their fluctuating moods and secretive glances at each other. She responds to this by providing food and leading the group in song after song as they cross the desert and prairie land. On the other hand, she also proves to be a frighteningly fast driver, almost an accident waiting to happen, which adds more suspense to a trip that is already fraught with tension.

Garwith's wife, Cicely, rail-thin but with an honest and open face, is slavishly devoted to her increasingly irascible husband. Doing what she can to make him happy, she is clueless about his criminal background and his plan to ultimately ditch her and run off with the money. She only knows that he is somehow dissatisfied with things and she is at a loss to make them better.

DELL FIRST EDITION B211

She made her way cross country with three men who had her—and murder—on their minds.

35¢

THE LONG RIDE

A James McKimmey Thriller

Then there is Vera Kennicot, the spinsterish librarian from Loma City. Depending on the taste of the reader, she is either very funny or very annoying. Big, loud, and decidedly unattractive, she is given to constantly quoting the classics and fidgeting with her AAA guidebook. Nakedly emotional, she immediately sets her cap for Benson, playfully punching and squeezing him, and insinuating herself into his presence. Reacting to her attentions as a man, Benson is both embarrassed and exasperated, he does his best to keep her at arm's length.

Finally, there is the lovely long-legged Margaret Moore. Slim and fine featured, she exhibits a calm and confident presence punctuated by a knowing intelligence and a throaty purr of a laugh. She and Benson are immediately drawn to each other and their quiet courtship provides him with needed respite from the tension of the investigation. And, yet, in the back of his mind, Benson wonders if she has any connection with Wells or Garwith and the missing satchel of Army cash. Needless to say, he hopes against anything that she doesn't.

As both the road trip and the novel move along, the reader is treated to short stays in Cheyenne, Laramie, and Reno, among other small towns and highway truck stops. Garwith has shipped the missing satchel ahead of them, addressing it to General Delivery at one post office after another. A succession of scenes has Garwith stealing away from the group's various lodgings to go see whether the package has been delivered or is still in transit. This often becomes a cat and mouse game where Wells, who has his eye on Garwith, tails him and waits to see if he takes possession of the swag. And tailing right behind him is Benson, who has his eye on both of them. Benson also has allies; other FBI agents stationed in each city who run interference at the post office or act as another pair of eyes when he can't watch both men at the same time.

Garwith eventually becomes wise to what Wells is about and that he is earnestly pursuing him. But he keeps this knowledge close to the vest, which adds to the story's tension, especially when the men have to verbally fence with each other in the car or under the lights of a motor court. Neither one is quite sure whether the other knows who they are. Garwith gradually sets his mind on some kind of escape; grabbing the loot for good and leaving everything behind, including his wife and Wells. He begins to fake illnesses and panic attacks, so that the group has to stay longer in some places, giving him a better opportunity to make his exit with cash in hand. At one point, he even cuts the station wagon's fuel line, causing it to stall in the middle of the desert.

For Wells, it's a simpler premise; recover the satchel and kill anyone who gets in his way. Initially focused solely on Garwith, he eventually realizes that Benson is after the money too, but without realizing why. Nevertheless, he continues his pursuit, undeterred, eventually leading to violent and disastrous consequences.

With **The Long Ride**, McKimmey has fashioned a unique crime story that has, as its backdrop, the changing landscape of the American highway. Added to this is a broad range of characters who are drawn into a succession of events that will leave all of them changed, for better or worse. Like most of McKimmey's novels, this one is written in the third person so the reader is afforded insights into each traveler's point of view at different times in the narrative. Moreover, he also takes the time to delve into their individual backgrounds and experiences; what moves them, what frightens them, and what makes them tick. Through this technique, McKimmey surprisingly creates empathy, and makes one want to know what will happen to each of them. Without a doubt, it's a long and perilous journey well worth taking.

Squeeze Play (1962), McKimmey's final entry in his Dell cycle, has much of the gambling milieu found in **Winner Take All** and uses its compulsions to fuel a tale of middle-class malaise. Jack Wade, professional engineer, is married to Binny, a troubled alcoholic and compulsive gambler. The tragic loss of their son has put her over the deep end. She is constantly leaving Jack to take impulsive bus rides up to Lake Tahoe and a local den of iniquity known simply as "The Casino." Not surprisingly, she runs up a lot of alcohol-tainted losses and empties their bank account. She's become an unreliable wife and an unfaithful one.

In this respect, she has been taken advantage of by a slick croupier in The Casino named Frank Delli, who sees her inebriated state almost every night. He sees Binny as not just an easy sexual conquest, but as bait and stooge for an elaborate ripoff scheme.

Jack Wade knows nothing about any scheme. What he does know is that his wife's reckless behavior is putting a chill in their marriage. It becomes worse when she calls him "Frank" while in an alcoholic haze and, worse still, when she suspects that she is pregnant with Frank's baby. Frantically trying to reconcile with Jack (so that he'll think the baby is his), she is unable to entice him back into bed. Reacting erratically to this rejection, she drinks even more than usual and abruptly steals what's left of their money. She gets back on the bus and rushes up to Tahoe, back to the dice and back to Frank.

Meanwhile, Jack Wade has much more to worry about. There's a new middle manager at his engineering firm, a manipulative glad-hander named Stan Harley, an idea stealer and an opportunist, who seizes every chance presented to criticize Jack in public and make him look bad to the firm's owner and CEO. Because of his wife's problems, Jack is driven to distraction, leaving him vulnerable to losing focus and making careless errors. Like any effective predator, Harley sees this and is ready to pounce on Wade whenever it's to his advantage to do so. Like many stressed-out professionals, Wade needs something or someone to help him relax and experience some warmth.

You guessed it, it's a beautiful woman, the new secretary in the office. McKimmey introduces us to Elaine Towne, a cool brunette in high heels and low-cut dresses. She starts giving Jack the quiet and warm attention he's been missing with Binny. He is drawn to her and tells himself that being with her is an almost sensuous experience, something he'd almost forgotten. And yet, as they have a few dates, it becomes clear that she is seducing Jack without giving him anything. Holding back enough with the promise of a passionate tryst, but never really delivering the goods. This keeps Jack interested but also keeps him on her string. So, if she doesn't want a real hot-blooded affair, what is it that she *does* want?

As it turns out, Elaine is in cahoots with Frank Delli, the croupier at The Casino. Knowing the dysfunctional marital connection between Binny and Jack, they've concocted a plan to rip off one of the "high rollers" who regularly patronizes Frank's roulette table, and use the couple as part of the bait and switch. Binny is, of course, the bait, and Frank convinces her to be the casino "date" and "luck" for one Charlie Wing, a boisterous Asian who likes to throw his money around and bet heavily, win or lose. Frank wants her to steer Wing to his wheel while allowing the gambler to ply her with drinks and plenty of betting money. What she doesn't know is that Frank's game will be rigged so that Wing will come away with an outsize wad of casino cash.

It doesn't take too much convincing to get Binny to go for this arrangement, but, curiously, she wants some assurance that she won't have to slip into bed with Wing at the end of the night. Frank quickly tells her not to worry, she's only to be Wing's companion in the casino and nowhere else. But as the night moves on and the dollars pile up, it's clear that Wing expects to have Binny for a celebratory dessert.

At the end of the night, with her scruples easily dissolved in a haze of alcohol, Binny leaves the casino with Wing to go to his motel. Inherently superstitious, he has abruptly quit gambling after seeing Frank abandon his table. The crooked croupier knows he will do this and he secretly observes Wing pick up his winnings and stuff them into a large money belt he wears under his clothes. Before he and Binny can go out into the cold Nevada night, Frank bolts from the casino and positions himself nearby, hidden from view and gripping a heavy tire iron.

In a truly frightening scene, he jumps out and beats them viciously, swinging the blunt shard of metal over and over again, until Wing and Binny have stopped moving and, incidentally, stopped breathing as well. Despite such sudden violence, Frank groans with orgasmic pleasure when he grabs Wing's money belt. He also has the presence of mind to move Binny's body to another location, which is an additional piece of the plan he and Elaine have cooked up together.

Meanwhile, Elaine has done her part by continuing her seduction of Jack. Out on a date, they have gone to the inevitable motel, and Jack has high expectations that the tryst she has been dangling in front of his hungry eyes for so long is finally imminent. Elaine drugs Jack, leaving him passed out on the motel bed, and creates a nice alibi by stepping out with a guy Jack knows from the engineering firm.

When Jack finally comes to, he awakens to the reality of being a patsy, the fall guy. Binny and Wing's bodies have been discovered and Jack is the chief suspect, neatly framed and now on the run from the police. Unlike **The Wrong Ones**, which is a "whodunit" until its very end, **Squeeze Play** is a "how's he gonna get out of it?" The balance of the novel deals with Jack's efforts to stay one step ahead of the cops, while simultaneously trying to find out who has suddenly made him a widower. He is aided in this effort by another woman, Helen Bartlett, his next door neighbor who is herself a widow. Helen has been aware of his trials with the alcoholic Binny and has sympathized with his plight. She continues to support him and believes his protestations of innocence.

Like the duplicitous Elaine, Helen is coolly attractive and Jack enjoys being in her presence. Unlike Elaine, she is genuine, caring, and stable, the mother of a young son. As she helps Jack elude the police, they are drawn closer together and eventually have a fervent affair, something that Elaine offered but never delivered.

Just what is it that gets Elaine off, what will heat her usually ice-cold blood? In a revealing scene, McKimmey provides the answer. When she gets together with Frank Delli and they plan their murderous scam, she dominates him in the same way that she manipulates Jack, with the promise of her heavenly body and all its delights. Frank responds eagerly with grandiose talk about all the money they will glom from the doomed Charlie Wing. He goes into it in detail and by counting the dollars even before they get them. All of this verbal finance actually gets Elaine visibly and sexually excited, and this turns Frank on even more. Money is the chink in her armor and it's not long before this couple from Hell consummate their perverse relationship.

With **Squeeze Play**, as in **The Long Ride**, McKimmey has provided us with a group of women who couldn't be more dissimilar and unlike each other; the doomed but still attractive alcoholic, Binny, the coldly venomous Elaine, and the naturally generous and warm-hearted Helen. Jack, as the middle-class Everyman, must deal with all of them in a dizzying succession of events that involve a crumbling marriage, theft, murder, and the desperate preservation of his own freedom. With such real-life characters and a plot full of surprises, this makes for another compelling story in the author's Dell First Edition series.

With this series, James McKimmey has created a solid body of original work, one that has aged well and justifiably commands attention. Seven self-contained novels, each readable on their own, but with thematic threads that emerge and reveal the writer's concerns: the suffocating small towns and their assumed expectations of conformity; the recurrent figure of the Outsider, who, intentionally or not, shakes up those towns and reveals their potential for sudden violence; the sexually charged relationships of men and women, and how they can be supportive or destructive; and the lure of easy money.

Moreover, McKimmey seasons his crime fiction (as the best of the genre's writers do) with social commentary: the dangers of mob justice; racial tension; the addictive potential of institutionalized gambling; and the role of the police, and their efforts, rightfully or wrongfully, to sort out the innocent from the guilty. McKimmey mixes all of these elements into a stew of sharp characterizations and plots that move, startle, and surprise. It is fortunate for aficionados of the genre that this Dell cycle, once the province of knowledgeable collectors, is now being republished (by Stark House Press) to a great degree for new readers and long-time fans alike. My advice? Don't hesitate to read the novels of James McKimmey.

• • •

Illustration by Carl Burgos (*Justice*, January 1956)

DIGGING INTO CRIME DIGESTS
James McKimmey at *Mike Shayne*
By Peter Enfantino

Thanks to Jeremy Burwell, we've already seen what James McKimmey could do with a novel-length thriller, but what about the author's forays into shorter work? According to the essential website, Galactic Central, McKimmey had nearly sixty stories appear in the digests between the years of 1957 and 1994, with the majority of those appearing in *Alfred Hitchcock's* and *Mike Shayne*. Though I don't rule out a future dissection of those *AHMM* tales, it's McKimmey's 21 *Shayne* contributions I'll be focusing on in this installment of Digging Into Crime Digests.

"A Decent Lie"
(November 1965; 3800 words) ★★★
    Golf is the root of all evil. Hal Beechum only wants to defeat his best pal and chief competitor, Maury Elstrom, in eighteen holes. Maury had recently become the first of the pair to record a 90 and Hal is convinced he can best that by ten. It certainly looks as though that's the case when, on the seventeenth, Hal shanks one into the trees and near the landscaper's shack. Approaching his ball (which happens to be perched upon a man's gold cap), he notices the corpse of an attractive woman, also clad in golf attire.
    Rather than ruin what will surely be a record-breaking day, Hal smacks the ball back on the course with an eye to reporting the fatality after the match. But when Hal heads back to the shack later, the body is gone. With a little amateur sleuthing, he discovers the identity of the killer and reports it to the police. Hilarious black comedy in which the game is king and paramount over anything, including murder. Not only does Hal resume his all-important game but, later, we discover the body is that of a nagging wife who insisted on playing golf with her husband . . . and then was beating him before the man wrapped a putter around her neck. The violence is all off-screen and the murder itself seems almost secondary to the sheer lunacy of the situation. McKimmey's *MSMM* debut is strong and assured and resembles some of the work he was pumping out for *Hitchcock's* at the time. Ordinary guys who become embroiled in situations they can't get out of without resorting to violence.

"The Hunted Ones"
(February 1966; 23,800 words) ★★

Billy and Maria are young and in love. Unfortunately, Maria's mother, Elizabeth Nivero, is a very powerful woman in San Lupe, and she's used to getting what she wants. What she wants right now is for her daughter to get on with high school and forget all about Billy Lang, but Billy's not playing along. When Elizabeth sends one of her security men to rough up Billy, the young hothead takes it personally; he talks Maria into hitting the road with him. So begins a very long chase that ends violently in Lake Tahoe. "The Hunted Ones" is, by far, the longest of McKimmey's stories to hit *Shayne*, but it's also the most simplistic and disposable. It's the same formula that would end up virtually every night on 1960s TV shows. Worse, the story is bloated, padded with inconsequential details that only add to the snail's pace.

"Search for an Achilles Heel"
(January 1967; 5800 words) ★★1/2

Though he created a fuse that netted his company a quarter-million dollars in sales, Emanuel Partridge has been frozen out of his own success. His boss, Laurence Dexter, owner of Dexter Products explains that Partridge signed a work-for-hire contract when he joined up years ago. Infuriated, the employee hatches a plan to net him some unflattering information on his boss, details he can use to blackmail Dexter into doing the right thing. The prose is a bit dry, but Partridge's plot is a fascinating and complex one; involving hidden microphones and a special device he invents to hook up to Dexter's typewriter, enabling him to read everything the boss types. In a hilarious scene near the climax, Dexter admits to stumbling across the device and patenting it, thus screwing Partridge out of yet another small fortune.

"Inside the Hidden Man"
(February 1967; 19,600 words) ★★★

Keith Craig seems to have what every seventeen-year-old boy wants: gorgeous girlfriend, a hot quarterback's arm, and bright future prospects. But an incident during a winning drive on the field, one that leaves an opposing player dead, seems to activate some kind of deep-seated hormone in Keith. He's killed and he likes it. Days later, he runs over a defenseless man on the side of the road and then cleans it up with the precision of a hitman. Keith's new-found love for violence reaches its apex when he robs a bank and murders three tellers in cold blood. Only an unbelieving sheriff stands between Keith Craig and his next victim.

Though I was let down by a weak climax (the sheriff and the kid have a showdown while McKimmey trots out the familiar psychology), "Inside the Hidden Man" is an enthralling road map from "cool jock" to "cold sociopath." An unflinching character study of a kid with something broken inside.

He kept remembering those eyes staring at him — in recognition?

He hesitated only a moment then took the pistol from the pocket of the raincoat and walked over to the man. He thumbed the safety off. He held the muzzle an inch from the man's temple. He fired. The sound of it seemed the roar of a cannon exploding.

The woman began struggling like a bound wild animal, her moaning much louder. He stepped over, pointed the pistol and fired again.

"Her World of Voices"
(June 1967; 1200 words) ★★

"Two Black Mantillas"
(September 1967; 2200 words) ★★1/2

Two stories that concern misdirected phone calls. In "Her World of Voices," Connie Adams, switchboard operator at a swanky uptown hotel, recognizes her ex-husband, Pete's voice when he asks for messages under an assumed name. Connie's marriage dissolved after she caught her ex with another woman under the same assumed name (dumb move that one), and the man has since remarried, so she suspects he's up to old tricks. When Pete's new wife calls looking for information, Connie is only too glad to provide it. In "Two Black Mantillas," control freak/physician Gregory Handwell keeps a tight leash on his wife, Phyllis, loading her up with errands and housework, while he meets frequently in Tijuana with his mistress. When Phyllis discovers the truth, Handwell is stopped at the border with a copious amount of illegal drugs in his glove compartment. Both stories prove two things: women are the more dangerous sex, and James McKimmey excels when given more room to stretch (as do most authors, I guess) and fill in the character gaps.

"The Quick Ambition of Bertram Wintroath"
(October 1967; 2600 words) ★★1/2

Bert Wintroath is a modestly successful underwriter at the Mayhew Insurance Company in San Francisco, but he has great taste in clothing, food, and women. In the latter department, Bert has been keeping time with the smolderingly beautiful Nina, but he has had just enough of her sense of humor and clinging ways. Just in the nick of time arrives Eloise Mayhew, daughter of the boss and just as smoking hot as Nina. Bert decides to trade up but Nina proves that a woman scorned and all that. Ironic and funny climax where Bert (literally) gets left holding the bag.

"Kill-Race"
(November 1967; 2800 words) ★★

Howie overhears his wife and her lover plot his untimely demise. The plan is to get Howie to agree to a race with "the other man" (who happens to have a very souped-up sports car) and then run his jalopy off the hairpin turn up at Highskill Road. But Howie has other ideas.

"Six Dead Man's Steps"
(December 1968; 1200 words) ★1/2
"The Loser"
(February 1969 1000 words) ★★

Two short-shorts with a similar theme. In "Six Dead Man's Steps," a detective must unmask the killer of a man who had just won big in Reno. The error the murderer makes is that the carpet had just been cleaned and his footprints were the only ones present.

"The Loser" finds a down-on-his-luck gambler wasting his life away playing Keno when he decides to rob a woman who's just won three grand. He kills the woman in the parking lot but is then shot by the police. Ironically, one of the cops finds a winning Keno sheet in the dead man's pocket. The climax is nicely ironic but highly implausible (how would a beat cop know this particular ticket was a winner?).

"Runners in the Park"
(April 1969; 4800 words) ★★★1/2

Vic Scanlon is a fat, misogynistic racist who uses his size to push around anyone who gets in his way. Lately, that's his pretty Mexican waitress, Constanza, who's been avoiding Vic's advances and double entendres since she first got the job. Tonight though, Vic is adamant: the girl must stay and have a steak with him after work and then they'll see what happens. Constanza protests that she's happily married and only wishes to continue her job at the cafe to help her husband, Jorge, through law school. When Vic turns violent, Costanza flees the diner into the awaiting car driven by Jorge. Later, Vic leaves the cafe and walks through the part of town he lives in, known as Devil's Park, with his entire week's cash intake in his pocket.

Vic almost relishes the idea of being jumped by one of the residents of the predominately Mexican neighborhood and is armed with a switchblade in case some action might pop up. He believes he sees someone following him and breaks into a run towards the shadow. When he catches up with the man, it turns out to be Jorge, who claims he was only in the park to think things over. Vic pulls his knife and tells Jorge he's going to cut him, but the younger man takes flight, heading into an abandoned house on the street. Knowing the house has been empty for years and there's no phone or electricity, Vic heads into the building with murder on his mind.

"Runners in the Dark" is a tense cat-and-mouse thriller with a brilliant twist ending and a truly evil lead character. Vic is almost a bi-polar creation; musing about how proud he is that his mortgage is almost paid off and segueing into white hot rage about the gentrification of Devil's Park. A multi-layered return to form for McKimmey.

"The Impersonation"
(September 1973; 4500 words) ★★★

Tired of a life gone wrong and get-rich-quick schemes that leave him penniless, Ralph Philbrook uses his gift for mimicry and a little greasepaint to become multi-millionaire J. Walter Talley for one quick trip to the bank. But one false move leaves Ralph handcuffed and headed for a long haul in the stir. A fun little heist yarn with a very clever reveal.

"The Bored Bunch"
(October 1973; 6000 words) ★★1/2

Surrounded by wealthy, arrogant friends, Richard Smitherton needs something to liven his boring life, so he begins stealing expensive items from his friends' collections. First, a necklace and earrings set, then a priceless painting, then his own wife's family flatware. The excitement generated within the circle is all he had hoped for and more, so he adds a new wrinkle: he returns the stolen merchandise and glows as he watches his friends' reactions. A bit of a slow grind, "The Bored Bunch" is saved by a fabulous last act, wherein Smitherton's friends decide not to contact their insurance companies about the returned valuables, thus welcoming them into the secret and intoxicating world of high society crime.

"A Record of Guilt"
(June 1975; 2700 words) ★1/2

Inspector Grange is sure old man Shrewer murdered Noel Berry but he can't prove it until he takes a walk on Shrewer's property with the neighbor's dog. Then all the pieces fall into place. Lazy, somnambulant short mystery patterned, no doubt, on the popular *Columbo* series, lacking any surprises. From the get-go, the Inspector suspects Shrewer and, by the end, he's got his man.

"The Mourning After"
(July 1976; 4700 words) ★★★1/2

Fired from a casino for cheating, loser Burt Rifkin finds himself bumming around the bars of Lake Tahoe aimlessly, until he meets Sherry Russell. Gorgeous and lively, Sherry is unlike any woman Burt has ever met and, very quickly, the two fall in love. At first everything is roses and money isn't even mentioned but then, one day, Sherry tells Burt she's bumped into an old friend who received an odd request. He's been hired to bump off an important man in town but Sherry talks Burt into intercepting the offer and up-front cash.

With the money comes instructions and an address. Burt and Sherry steal a car and park in a grove near the target's place. Burt heads in, murders the man, and races back to the grove, where he discovers Sherry and the car are gone. In a panic, he heads back to his apartment and waits on word from the woman, even though he knows deep down Sherry has run some kind of con on him. The next day Burt discovers the murdered man was Paul Angel, owner of the Mountain Club, a very popular casino in Tahoe. The next day, Angel's rival, Laurence Marquart, is found dead, the apparent victim of a revenge/retaliation by Angel's crew.

Burt has a brilliant idea and visits the mortuary holding Marquart's services. There at the coffin of the dead man, is Sherry. Burt approaches her and she accuses him of murdering her lover, Marquart. Sherry confesses that she set Burt up to murder Angel and that her next move will be to silence Burt forever. Panicked, Burt places his gun in Marquart's dead hand, hides the weapon in the desert and then makes an anonymous tip to the police. They arrest Burt the same day, explaining that Sherry told them the whole story (well, a *new* story) about Burt's involvement in both murders. When Burt asks about the fingerprints on the gun, he's told that Marquart had no use of the hand the fingerprints came from. Now, Burt sits in prison waiting for a shiv from a hired killer.

More than any other of the *MSMM* appearances, "The Mourning After" feels like a McKimmey creation. There's the pitch, the con, the betrayal, and the after-effects that McKimmey played to perfection in his crime novels. Stepping foot into Jim Thompson territory, there's the hapless (some might say brainless) Burt Rifkin, who can't catch a break no matter how it's handed to him, can't resist a beautiful broad with a plan, and has that classic quick temper that usually translates to death or hard time. McKimmey hints that Marquart was offed by Angel's men but it's never declared so the climax is nicely ambiguous.

"The Crimes of Harry Waters"
(May 1977; 4800 words) ★★★
　　With his welfare checks drying up, (unpublished) poet Harry Waters is finding it hard to make ends meet. After a long conversation with himself, Harry decides that prison might be the best place to be. Three solid meals a day and a roof over his head. Problem is, Harry literally can't get arrested. He robs a grocery store (and is then told "thank you" by the owner, who hangs the theft around his lazy son-in-law's neck), puts a brick through a Rolls-Royce windshield (and is then told "thank you" by the owner who can now get a brand new windshield through his insurance), and attempts to sexually assault a young lady (who takes Harry's act as a compliment). No prison time.
　　Growing desperate, Harry assaults a police officer in full view of a squad car and then learns that the cop whose nose he busted is a fraud casing a business for a robbery. Harry gets a fifteen thousand dollar reward! Now, Harry decides he can relax and enjoy life. That's when the IRS knocks at his door and the agents tell him he's going to jail for tax fraud for not reporting his reward! Hilarious and ironic, with some laugh-out-loud sequences and dialogue, in particular the scene where Harry has climbed a trellis to break in on the pretty girl. He never intends to rape the woman, but he's hoping she sees that as the intention and calls the police. She doesn't:

"Why did you come up here like this?"
"Because you're so beautiful and desirable looking."
"Most of them just buy me expensive dinners and things and think they're proving something. I've never been fooled, you know."
"I'm certain you haven't been."
"But you truly proved you mean it. The risk!"

"I should be put in solitary."
"Come over here," she said.
"What?"
She switched out the light. "I said come over here."
"Right now?"
"Faster than that if you can."

"The Peace Monger "
(February 1978; 6200 words) ★★1/2
　　Black comedy about a Nobel Peace Prize winner who turns to violence after his neighbors start blasting heavy metal music all night long. The concept is amusing but the story is padded and contains a couple of drawn-out phone conversations and some speculation on the death of the writer's wife a year before.

"Where There's a Will"
(June 1978; 6200 words) ★★★
　　With insurance money on the line, Susan Adams heads back home to make sure neither her stepmother nor brother get their hands on the cash. When she discovers, to her glee, that her father had not rewritten his will when he'd remarried and named his new wife, Molly, the beneficiary, Susan knows the only obstacle to the green is her weak brother, Mark. Years before, Mark had attempted suicide but Susan had talked him out of it (to her eternal chagrin). The bright side is that Mark had written a suicide note and Susan had tucked that away for safe keeping.
　　She arrives at Mark's place to find a stranger in a wheelchair opening the door. He introduces himself as Mark's "very close friend" Richard Bennington, and informs Susan that Mark is out of town on business but expected back any minute. Though Susan has her suspicions about this man she's never heard of before, she lets the situation ride, biding her time until Mark gets back and she can finish *her* business.
　　But once she settles in, Susan begins to worry. Richard has locked and bolted all the doors and the windows have been nailed down and, for a gay man, he sure is taking in the sights. After she drinks a cup of coffee, Susan passes out for hours, waking to discover her purse (with the

note) is missing. When she confronts Richard, he confesses to the frightened woman that he is actually the step-brother Susan never bothered to meet. Together, he and his mother, Molly, have planned the death of both Susan and Mark. Susan busts through the glass of the back door and begins to climb through when she hears footsteps behind her and turns to discover that Richard isn't as helpless as he appeared.

A well-paced thriller, "Where There's a Will" could have made for a nifty little ABC Movie of the Week (as could so many of McKimmey's thrillers), with Susan making for a particularly nasty protagonist who falls into a fatal trap of her own making. How can the reader squirm and feel sympathy for a woman who came home to kill her brother? Though I guessed the walking status of "crippled" Richard very early on, McKimmey's finale is still a chiller:

"Susan?" he called again, and now she heard something other than his voice.

It was the sound of his shoes striking the linoleum of the kitchen as he ran to catch her.

"Where There's a Will" is a perfect example of the detour that *Mike Shayne* had taken in the mid to late 1970s, steering itself away from the dying world of espionage and clunky PI fiction and re-entering the waters of the straight-ahead crime thrillers that had made the digest such a force in its early days. The issue also featured the first (of eight) stories for *Shayne* written by Joe R. Lansdale, an author who would become well known for just the type of thrillers McKimmey was writing.

"Pigeons"
(January 1979; 3100 words) ★★★
Bird-watcher Maudie Adams is appalled to discover the jerk living next to her is shooting birds with his shotgun. Henry Willtz's sadistic hobby has been brought on by Maudie's refusal to marry him. One day, while Maudie is walking the lane, Henry shoots down a pigeon belonging to the "new guy" on the block: Edward Gornish a young grad student down at the University. Oddly enough, the dead bird has a small sack tied to one of its legs and, upon closer inspection, Maudie and Henry notice a small piece of glass inside the bag. Remembering the recent rash of jewels stolen from the University museum, Maudie deducts that Gornish is using the pigeon to smuggle the baubles back to his house.

Killing two birds with one stone (yes, I pun), Maudie makes an anonymous call to the police, informing them that Wiltz and Gornish are partners in the robberies. Soon, Maudie is alone on her street, peacefully watching birds from her porch bench. An entertaining short "cozy" with a snappy conclusion.

"The Bus That Disappeared"
(May 1979; 10,800 words) ★1/2
A bus carrying eight passengers from the Sunset Mobile Home Park in San Francisco is forced off the road and down a rocky cliff, leaving all aboard relatively unharmed but lost to the outside world. But when the bus driver discovers the steering mechanism was tampered with, the question becomes: did someone want one of the riders onboard dead? Each character has their own nuances and background, and none seem to get along. Can this group of survivors somehow band together and work towards eventual rescue?

"The Bus That Disappeared" most closely resembles an ABC Movie of the Week with its low-impact danger and cliched characters. The final outcome and reveal of who the target was and why they were targeted is almost laughable. Given the space allotted the story, this is a huge disappointment.

"The Bus Stops Here"
(January 1985; 3000 words) ★★★
Six years later, James McKimmey returns for his last story to appear in *MSMM*, which also features a busload of senior citizens. Well, 37 of them are elderly, but on this latest trip the regulars seem to have an invader in their midst: an arrogant young man who's decided that, on this, his 21st birthday, no one will tell him what to do.

And the problem is that he's sitting in Ben Oldfield's chair. After a heated discussion, Ben decides to sit in another seat but he realizes that this day will not end well. The bus reaches its destination of Reno and the passengers all disembark to spend their limited funds (and eight hours) trying to beat the one-armed bandit.

Ben has always been a good card counter and never leaves the casino without a modest profit, but the kid is getting on his nerves. The young man seemingly cannot lose at whatever he tries his hand at, and now he's decided to sit down at the same blackjack table and completely screw Ben's concentration. The old man loses everything and is confined to the worst place possible in a Nevada casino: the lobby. Whispers go through the crowd of seniors that the kid is up one hundred grand. When the bus rolls out of the parking lot once their eight hours is up, the kid's laden not just with greenbacks but with a cute girl as well

That's it, decides Ben, who orders the bus driver to stop at the bridge. Hours later, the detectives are still trying to sort out why the young couple jumped. With "The Bus Stops Here," James McKimmey seems to have rediscovered what made his early novels and short fiction such compulsive reading: that edge, that sense that something nasty could happen at any moment. The climax might make you laugh, but then think hard on the fact that 37 passengers and a bus driver all conspired to murder these two youngsters simply because of a bit of arrogance.

• • •

Caroline Munro
FIRST LADY OF FANTASY

The Spy Who Loved Me Contact Sheet

85

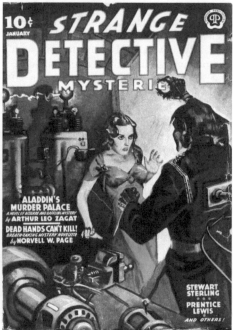

S. Craig Zahler on . . . Pulps

Adventure
May 1st 1931

During my explorations of the pulpwood vastness, I read the May 1st 1931 issue of the *Adventure* pulp magazine. This highly regarded publication is loaded with tales that were written by actual adventurers and well-traveled, worldly experts of that era. So yes, this publication is less "pulpy" than my favorite pulp magazines — *The Spider*, *Operator #5*, *Dime Detective*, *Weird Tales*, and *Terror Tales* — but I do not use the term "pulpy" in a pejorative sense, though many do. Melodrama and implausibility often cause something to feel "pulpy," but for me, creativity and passion regularly trump realism, so I enjoy reading fiction with a "pulpy" approach. (Norvell W. Page, Clark Ashton Smith, H.P. Lovecraft, Max Brand, Donald Wandrei, Bruno Fischer, and David Goodis are some of my favorite authors.)

This May 1, 1931 issue was my first experience with *Adventure*, though I have read two good books culled from this magazine: one by Harold Lamb (**Durandal**) and the other by J. Allan Dunn (**Barehanded Castaways**). I had only finished a fraction of this pulp issue before I had ordered another. The verisimilitude does make some of these tales very vivid, and the breadth of the publication is quite impressive.

Of course, the stories vary in quality, though there is no bad or even mediocre material (excepting perhaps the one incomplete serial, which I did not read). There are some light trifles (e.g. "What No Sound?"), some short and informative nonfiction pieces, some more substantial stories that detail an event or two ("The Laughing Fox," about seal hunters, and "Two Rounds," about military frugality), and then the two much bigger tales ("Jiggers" and "Bush Devils"), which prove to be the unquestionable highlights.

The few negative comments I have for the magazine (which is 192 double column pages in small type, so around 400 trade paperback pages) have to do with the quantity of okay or unadventurous material that lie between the glossy ends. The few trifling stories do not enhance the reading experience overall, though the letter column and short nonfiction articles do. Additionally, some of the stories lack adventure — Georges Surdez's very, very predictable French Legion tale and Ganpat's "Two Rounds" are really just an event or two in a remote location and are not especially transporting. Both could have been in a war magazine, and lack the spirit of adventure.

The highly regarded author Talbot Mundy provides a decent pirate story called "Black Flag," but the tale seems like the condensed version of a much more substantial story and is awkwardly paced (and contains a surfeit of nautical terms). As is, the frequent switches in perspective and the oddly summarized incidents make it feel like the retelling of a longer tale and somewhat incomplete, though it has its moments and a couple of laughs.

The two best stories in the issue wholly validate reading all of the other decent, albeit unexceptional, material.

Arthur O. Friel, who was admired by many (including Robert E. Howard), delivers a big novelette adventure called "Bush Devils," wherein an explorer and a troubled guide hunt diamonds in the jungle while cowing some indigenous folks. This is very vivid adventuring, written by a man who lived this sort of thing, and the questions about the characters' motives are also quite compelling. I've been a fan of Robert E. Howard for 30 years, but his stories seem simple and sparse compared to something like "Bush Devils." (I imagine all Howard fans would like this story, even though it does not have a fantasy element.)

Then there is "Jiggers" by L. Patrick Greene. Why isn't this terrific English author much better known? The narrative of this African treasure hunt is interestingly arranged, has a great trajectory, and works very well as an allegory without being pedantic. And like the other material of Greene that I've read (his wonderful, funny, and well-plotted stories of The Major), "Jiggers" displays a good sense of humor and an interesting exploration of race relations as well as some fine ruminations about the adventurer's psyche. There are surprises at every plot point, and the author puts the reader on the front line of this fast moving and obliquely told tale of greed and providence. Like "Bush Devils," "Jiggers" is a complete and transporting success, and another reason that I will read more issues of *Adventure*.

Strange Detective Mysteries
January 1941

I purchased this *Strange Detective Mysteries* pulp from 1941 because of the cover story by my favorite writer, Norvell W. Page (The Spider, **But Without Horns**, etc.), but his convoluted tale of suburban yellow peril wound up being the least compelling of the bunch (and loaded with a ton of forced exposition at its conclusion). Still, all Page tales that I've read have value, and this one did feature a character named "Chichester" and some very memorable head injuries. Henry Kuttner supplies a short dreamy tale like something Paul Ernst might have supplied to *Weird Tales*, and R.S. Lerch

provides a paranoiac and smelly tale that is a bit too condensed and contrived for its duration, though it is decent. Although judging a book or pulp by its cover is not advisable, with this issue, you can certainly judge a story by its title — the two highlights are very well named . . .

"Case of the Growing Corpse" (Stewart Sterling) is equally puzzling and disgusting, and seems a bit like a precursor to '80s splatterpunks like Shaun Hutson. Ever read a story with a severed arm that is slowly growing in size? Read this . . . and be ready for gross bewilderment.

"Beware the Blind Killer!" is by Bruno Fischer (writing as Russell Gray). Like pretty much everything I've read by this talented guy, it is intense, surprising, dark, and exciting. It has both a nasty edge and some interesting and morally gray internal conflicts for the protagonist (especially for a borderline shudder/horror pulp). In this story, the main character is a cop whose wife may be a murderer. The title describes the weirder aspect of the tale and is quite deserving of its exclamation point. Oddly, this story best delivered the darkness, mania, and intensity I was expecting from Norvell W. Page, and alongside Sterling's story, makes the issue worth seeking out, especially since everything is engaging at some level.

The Clipper Menace (The Skipper)
July 1937

The Skipper is a lesser-known pulp hero magazine that (alphabetically) fits between *The Shadow* and *The Spider*, which was perhaps a newsstand idea, but aesthetically reads like a bloody noir version of Doc Savage. I've read LOTS of *The Spider* and *Operator #5* pulps, both of which I favor over my samplings of *Doc Savage* (clever, but a bit too cloying and cute) and *The Shadow* (often too sloppy or overwritten, even by pulp standards), and The Skipper has the violence of those earlier Popular Publications, but the bickering team antics that appear in Doc. Fortunately, *The Skipper*'s supporting cast is not a homogeneous bunch of "comedic" scientist goofs, which is a chief complaint I have with Doc Savage, but a group of different and very complementary characters. More than anything, this rag-tag bunch reminds me of Jimmie Cordie's band of rogues, whose very enjoyable adventures were published in *Argosy* and *Frontier* pulps (and are equally recommended). And that is another thing that this novel and its backup stories have more than do most hero pulps: adventure.

The Skipper: **The Clipper Menace** rivals many of the better issues of *The Spider* and *Operator #5* in terms of overall quality. The paranoiac atmosphere of those pulps is here and the lethal violence as well, though not on as grand a scale or quite as nasty. And while the character of the The Skipper/ Captain John Fury may not be much better defined than that of Jimmy Christopher/ Operator #5, the former protagonist has a hard-edged noir attitude and feels far more multi-dimensional than does Operator #5, who is a good and practically flawless savior. The Skipper is not bananas like Norvell W. Page's The Spider, but he feels like a guy who might have existed and did his best with what he had.

The Skipper has personality, and this book has logical, albeit convoluted plotting (very much like *Operator #5* in this regard), rich atmosphere, a sense of adventure, and a really, really exceptional vehicle. "Whirlwind" is The Skipper's highly weaponized tanker that he and his team use out in the pacific to figure out why bodies are dropping from the sky and look for Gold Island. Also, the ice torture sequence certainly smells and feels a lot like the master of mania, Norvell W. Page. Before I'd finished this strong pulp hero adventure, I'd ordered another issue, as well as *The Whisperer*, which was also written by Lawrence Donovan.

The Red Invader (Operator #5)
by Frederick C. Davis (as Curtis Steele)

After reading seven Operator #5 novels, **The Red Invader** stands out as the best, slightly beating out the nastiest, which is **Master of Broken Men**. Frederick C. Davis is very well liked in pulp circles, and I definitely like a ton of what he does here (and in the Operator #5 books **Green Death Mists** and **Blood Reign of the Dictator**, which are almost as good).

My one complaint with his writing (here and elsewhere) is that his action sequences are written like sloppy book reports — there is information, but no flow, and he regularly substitutes the word "as" for the word "and" as if they are wholly interchangeable. His action lacks the sense of timing and spatial orientation that exists in the works of Max Brand, Robert E. Howard, and the #1 master of action, Norvell W. Page, and even second tier guys like Paul Chadwick (Secret Agent X) and Emile C. Tepperman (the second Operator #5 writer) provide clearer action.

Regardless of that criticism, I am a big fan of Frederick C. Davis, who in this adventure (and others) exceeds most if not all of his hero pulp contemporaries in three big ways

1. Intelligent tactics. The bad guys have good plans, not just "consolidate the bad guys" or "poison gas guns." And thus, the plans of the good guys must be similarly smart.

2. Expert escalation of tension. **The Red Invader** should be taught in a course entitled, "How to Gradually Build Tension from Page 1 until The End." The plotting is sharp, purposeful, and suffocating in this tale.

3. An abundance of believable details. The weaponry and foes described in this adventure feel authentic, and the main weapon is a truly harrowing threat.

I can honestly say that I am not sure which of the historical footnotes about weapons and politics are fact and which are fiction. This blurry line also helps sell the story's big ideas.

Do you want to read a tense, paranoia-inducing, grandly explosive, xenophobic, expertly-plotted war fever dream? Read **The Red Invader**.

Satan Paints the Sky (G-8 and His Battle Aces #52)
by Robert J. Hogan

The bad guy has a dagger stuck in his head. The point is in his brain and the hilt is just sticking out there. He's not very happy about this . . . but I am.

Although there is far more to this book

than this particularly strong visual idea, this idea is really something. (This is shown on both the cover and the very first page of the story, so I'm not spoiling anything.)

Recommended in Ed Hulse's indispensable **The Blood 'N' Thunder Guide To Collecting Pulps**, the aeronautical adventure of G-8 entitled **Satan Paints the Sky** is a nearly perfect example of how a few strong visual ideas (there are others besides the villain, especially one involving picnic baskets), some especially fluid/invisible prose, and a particularly well turned plot can be all that is required for an engaging reading experience. The various plot inversions are logical but rarely foreseeable, especially at the speed that Robert J. Hogan moves this WWI flying spy tale.

I've enjoyed the other G-8 adventures that I've read, but this one compares to my hero pulp favorites, The Spider and Operator #5.

The Blood 'N' Thunder Guide to Pulp Fiction by Ed Hulse

Although online searches and stumbling through websites can unearth a wealth of information on many subjects, I like to reward individuals who go through the extra effort of writing, laying out, and printing a book on whichever subject I'm interested in researching. I've purchased guides on progressive rock albums, television horror movies from the seventies, direct-to-video cult films, Western television shows of the fifties and sixties, American martial arts films, country music, anime, heavy metal, soul music, and other niche subjects. Not until I read **The Blood 'N' Thunder Guide to Pulp Fiction** had I read a guide that intelligently and tastefully delivered the promise of its premise.

As a longtime fan of H.P. Lovecraft, Clark Ashton Smith, Robert E. Howard, Max Brand, Edgar Rice Burroughs, Isaac Asimov, and David Goodis, I had hoped that a guide on pulp magazines would reveal to me some lesser known, but comparably skilled authors from the pulp milieu. This information lies in great abundance in Ed Hulse's book. Although I have not read this tome cover to cover, I have read the major part of the book, and many of the chapters multiple times. The wit and good taste that the author shows when discussing the subject of pulp fiction led to my discovery of scores of forgotten works that deserve rediscovery.

This valuable guide is neither the slobbering work of a rabid fan who likes everything, nor the work of a snobby elitist who feels superior to the material about which he writes, but a collection of smart, zesty essays — arranged by genre — of somebody who appreciates the varied aims of various pulp magazines. The rich and meticulously crafted tales of the stately *Adventure*, the apocalyptic visions of *Operator #5*, the hyperventilating bloody mania of *The Spider*, the aggressive modes of detection employed by those fellas in *Dime Detective*, the depravity of the Red Circle shudder pulps, the grandeur of *Astounding Stories*, the eldritch charms of *Weird Tales*, and the merits of many other genres and subgenres are critically and fondly discussed by the wellspring of pulp knowledge that is Ed Hulse. Wanna know which pulps to read as the best of their genre? Follow the advice of Mr. Hulse. Wanna know which exact issues of each magazine are the exemplars? Follow the advice of Mr. Hulse. Wanna know about the evolution of a particular magazine or genre? Get this book.

By heeding the thoughtful words of this sage of the yellow page, I have bettered my library and life and altered my list of favorite authors. Thank you, Mr. Hulse for opening the pulpwood door behind which stand such incredible talents as Norvell W. Page, Bruno Fischer, Arthur O. Friel, L. Patrick Greene, Harold Lamb, Frederick C. Davis, D.L. Champion, and many others . . .

• • •

SLEAZE ALLEY

Reviews by Peter Enfantino

THE GIRL OF HIS DREAMS WAS A GOLD PLATED NIGHTMARE!

$20 LUST

By ANDREW SHAW

50¢

NB 1546

S¹

THIS IS AN ORIGINAL NIGHTSTAND BOOK

$20 Lust
by Andrew Shaw (Lawrence Block)
Nightstand, February 1961
Cover Artist: Harold W. McCauley
Sex: ★1/2
Story: ★★★1/2
Cover: ★★1/2

Long before Lawrence Block was a well-respected and best-selling author, he paid some of his bills much the same way as other struggling soon-to-bes like Hunter, Silverberg, and Whittington. In Block's afterward to a reprinting/retitling of **$20 Lust**, published by Subterranean Press under the more respectable **Cinderella Sims**, the author dismissed the work as "utter crap." **$20 Lust/Cinderella Sims** was originally designed to be Block's sophomore Gold Medal novel (following the classic **Mona**) until the young writer "lost faith in it" and dumped it in the lap of Greenleaf in 1961. It was Block's 11th Greenleaf title (all published under the Nightstand Library imprint), and one he really shouldn't have been ashamed of.

After his wife leaves him and then dies in a fiery car crash, newspaperman Ted Lindsay quits his job and drinks himself from Louisville to New York. The days fly by Ted in a boozy haze until one day he glances a woman on the street and falls madly in love at first sight. Using his reporter brain, Ted is able to track the woman to a small apartment just down the street from his flop. He reads the woman's postal box and the name there, Cinderella Sims, intrigues the man even more. A new lease on life, Ted puts the booze on hold and begins monitoring the woman's every move on the street, through binoculars, from his apartment window. Then one day, while Ted is looking for traces of Cinderella in her apartment, he discovers she's even closer: right behind his back, holding a gun on him.

The gorgeous gal demands to know what Ted's up to with his daytime stalking and he sputters out a mostly-true reply. After his oratory is finished, Sims lowers her gun and explains that she's on the run from a Nevada mobster named Reed and his hoods. Cindy was a bad girl and stole fifty large from the man during a con game. She's been hopping from state to state since. Ted offers Cindy a helping hand in exchange for half the dough and she happily agrees. They seal the deal with a hot lay.

Very soon, Ted begins to regret the rash decision he's made. Ted talks Cindy into running away to Phoenix and starting a new life with the stolen loot but before they can get away, they discover Reed and his goons outside the apartment. Trouble is, Ted and Cindy are outside as well. Ted manages to overpower one of the men and get inside, grab the bag of money, and then meet up with his new squeeze down the road. They hop that plane to Phoenix and arrive in one piece, ready to change names and atmosphere.

But something doesn't sit right with Ted. Why would Reed spend an inordinate amount of money and time just to get fifty grand? His suspicions lead him to a local bank, where he offers up one of the twenties from the bag to a clerk. Telling the man he just thought the bill was funny-looking, Ted asks him to check it for counterfeit. After a few minutes, the man returns, telling Ted he's got one hell of a good eye: "Wouldn't have spotted it myself!"

A frazzled and angry Ted suddenly wonders what else Cinderella Sims has been lying about. Turns out the lovely lass stole the funny money and intends to sell it back to Reed for a hundred grand. But why would Reed pay double what it's worth? Because he's making an even better version of the bill and he doesn't want any of the old stuff in circulation to alert the Feds. That's also why he wants Cindy dead. Suddenly smelling a whole lot more free dough, Ted talks Sims into traveling to Reed's home base in San Francisco to steal the plates, printing press, and the whole nine yards. But that's not all, assures Ted. He doesn't want to be looking behind him for the rest of his life. Reed and his boys have gotta go.

$20 Lust is the oddest Greenleaf I've read (well, outside of that Silverberg splatter novel — Lust Crew — reviewed in bare•bones #1) and really the first that I've thought could easily have been published by a mainstream publisher like Gold Medal or Dell. There's barely any sex to speak of and Block's descriptions of the couplings are not what you'd classify as even soft core:

I took her breasts in my hands and stroked them. I never knew anything could be so soft, so firm and so perfect. I ran my lips over each breast in turn, tasting the flavor of her, kissing the firm pink nipples that stood up like little toy soldiers.

She was wearing white silk panties and I could see right through them.

Then she wasn't wearing anything at all.

No, the emphasis here is clearly not on the sighs but the surprise. Block does a wonderful job of continually conning the reader while his characters con each other. Cinderella Sims changes her shades more than the chameleon, from innocent to menacing to sly seductress to reluctant participant in murder. Even more fascinating is Ted's transformation from grieving barfly to cold-blooded killer. It's in that grim final act, where Ted and Cindy travel to the Bay Area to finish the job, that Block reminds us why he's a master of suspense and pacing. Ted's brutality in the finale is unflinching and uncharacteristic of a "porn" novel, as in this passage where one of the hoods, trussed up and out of answers, begs Ted to kill him quickly and painlessly:

> *"How do you want it?"*
> *"A bullet."*
> *I shook my head, hating myself. "I don't want to risk the noise."*
> *"Muffle it with a pillow."*
> *I shook my head.*
> *"Then hit me," he said. "Knock me out. Then any way you want. Just quick and easy, that's all."*
> *"Close your eyes."*
> *He closed them. I took the gun from Cindy, reversed it, gave him the butt across the front of the skull.*

In his foreword to that Subterranean Press volume, our much-missed friend, Ed Gorman, speaks highly of Lawrence Block's sleaze output: *I read three of his erotic novels and I'll tell you something. They're better written (and we're talking 1958-61) than half the contemporary novels I read today. He was pushing against form even back then, creating real people and real problems, and doing so in a simple powerful voice that stays with you a hell of a long time.* Ed's right on the money. It's mind-boggling that a fine crime novel like **$20 Lust** was consigned to truck stops and sex shops and not given a proper "airing" like the John D. MacDonalds or Richard Starks. According to Bob Speray's essential website (*greenleaf-classics-books.com*), Block wrote 29 novels for Greenleaf, and those not wanting to shell out the big bucks for the originals can find several of these (including **Cinderella Sims**) available as e-books on Amazon.

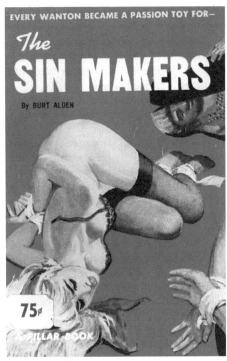

EVERY WANTON BECAME A PASSION TOY FOR—

The **SIN MAKERS**
By BURT ALDEN

75¢

A PILLAR BOOK

The Sin Makers
by Burt Alden (Richard A. Curtis)
Pillar, September 1963
Cover Artist: Robert Bonfils
Sex: ★★
Story: ★★1/2
Cover: ★★★

Joseph Irving Jelesco (Jij to his friends) has discovered his wife, Corliss, is having an affair with their interior decorator and elicits advice from his partner, Kelsey (the two form the partnership, Jaykay Originals, manufacturers of snazzy women's sportswear). Problem is, Jij has never been one to show patience. On this day, he walks into Kelsey's office while his partner is bonking their secretary, Rina:

> *There is something immensely appealing about a girl in high heels, lacy bra and panties who is struggling to get a dress over her head. Maybe its her total defenselessness. Yes, I guess that's it. She looked as vulnerable as the Maginot Line did in 1939, and the more I looked at her wriggling out of that tight style 600 — I told that goddamn designer fifty times to move the neck button lower — the more I felt like the Panzer division.*

93

After giving Jij a good show, Kelsey inquires as to what is so important that he should interrupt a business meeting. Jij explains his marital woes and admits that he intends to murder the decorator and then divorce his wife, Corliss. Kelsey calmly explains that the law frowns on murder and talks his friend into something a little more . . . fun.

The pair head to Jij's house with a camera, chloroform, adhesive tape, infrared bulbs, and a coffin. Perfect ingredients for a raucous party, no? They catch Corliss and her beau in mid-ecstasy and break into the house, donning monkey masks. The lovers are so fixated on climax that they have no idea what's going on and before they know it, the chloroform has been applied. With the help of Kelsey, Jij tapes the two adulterers together tightly and drops them into the coffin. Next stop: the steps of the Museum of Natural History.

The partners decide they're bored with their exorbitant lives; they liquidate the business and hop a plane for exotic locales. To Kelsey, it's just more of the same but to Jij, who's been faithful to his wife the last eight years, it's the starving man at the buffet. Jij is amazed by his friend's prowess:

Jij was like a starved shark who finds himself off Jones Beach on a Sunday in August. I've never seen anyone gratify any appetite as thoroughly, as abandonedly, as voraciously as he did. He went from woman to woman, black to white to brown to yellow, domestic to import, wealthy to penniless, stunning to ghastly, like a queen bee in a honeycomb, if you'll pardon the switch in gender. He left a trail of panting bodies that would stretch from Cuba to Miami if placed end to end and if they floated. He strew his seeds like some Caribbean Cadmus, and it wouldn't surprise me if a hundred illegitimate Jelescos now populated the region.

After a bit of island-hopping, they settle on the intriguingly-named Mocos Verdes ("Green Snot"), a Caribbean island lorded over by the "rat-faced" Benjamin Quimsby. The allure of Mocos Verdes is that the island is populated by love-starved native girls with nary a man in sight. After a grueling boat trip, the boys land on the beach of MV and are greeted by the creepy Mr. Quimsby, who offers Jij and Kelsey a room at his posh hotel, and Quimsby's gorgeous and well-built daughter, Dessa (*her breasts rose robustly off the surface of her chest the way Popocateptl and Ixtacihuad spring from the Mexican plains*). Quimsby makes it very clear that every woman on the island is at the boys' disposal . . . except Dessa. Despite the subtle warning, Kelsey makes it clear to Dessa he wants to know her more intimately, and it's very evident that the feeling is mutual. The two consummate their passion later on a a surfboard.

While making post-coital small talk, Dessa allows how she's always wanted to bring her nasty pop down to earth and wring him dry of his riches. Together, Dessa and Kelsey hatch a plan: with Jij involved, the trio will form a partnership and open a garment factory right there on the island. Once the business is up and running, they assume rather optimistically, they'll run Quimsby out of business and right off the island.

Unfortunately, it doesn't go as planned since Quimsby seems to always be one step ahead of the boys, crushing each move Jij and Kelsey make. That may be due to the fact that Dessa is a double-agent, working for her pop to put the JayKay team out to pasture. In the end, the new company faces bankruptcy and Quimsby makes the boys a fair offer to amscray.

The Sin Makers begins intriguingly and author Richard Curtis keeps the prose peppered with enough humor so as to distract from the fact there is no real plot to speak of. Problem is, once the partners hit Mocos Verdes, the novel becomes more of a syllabus on creating a garment manufacturing business, interspersed with anemic sexual escapades. It's tough to recommend this one but I found so much of the prose laugh-out-loud funny that it's worth the slog through the business tutoring. I doubt the one-handed readers of 1963 found it stimulating. Author Richard A. Curtis wrote four other Greenleafs, all in the course of one year: **Lust Pro** (Midnight Reader, December 1962, as by John Dexter), **Jet Set Sinners** (Leisure, November

1963, as by Curt Aldrich), **Sin Sell** (Pillar, November 1963, as by Burt Alden), and **Passion Spree** (Pillar, December 1963, as by Burt Alden).

Shame Street
by Don Holliday
Pillar, September 1963
Cover Artist: Robert Bonfils
Sex: ★★★
Story: ★★★
Cover: ★★★

28-year-old virgin Donald Spaulding has decided this weekend is the time to become a man. No more stroke books or stag films, he's going to make love to a real live woman for the first time in his life. Donald's a public accountant, makes a good wage, and has been saving up for just this sort of weekend, so he stashes his dough in his wallet and heads out the door to the first bar he sees, *The Hole*.

Just so happens that *The Hole* is the hangout for a tight-knit group of characters who are more than willing to open up their exclusive guest book for Don, who's flashing his green in public almost as much as resident prostitutes, Maybelle and Arlene, flash their breasts. The guys who frequent the bar stools at *The Hole* include: recently single Ben Flake, who treats women like punching bags and has the supreme goal of becoming wealthiest pimp in the neighborhood; Tommy Haze, who's just a week away from a stint in the joint and wants this to be his "lost weekend," three days of debauchery that will tide him over for the next few years of celibacy; and Fat Daddy, the neighborhood's pusher, who excels at hooking youngsters on 'H' and then raising the price.

Thanks to a night with Maybelle, Don discovers he's more well-endowed than just about any other guy out there and can perform like a race horse:

"Gee, I never knew making love was so good," Spaulding said. "I think I'll probably make love all the time from now on. Maybe I'll even get a girl to live with me." He was quite sober now and had taken the tie from his forehead.

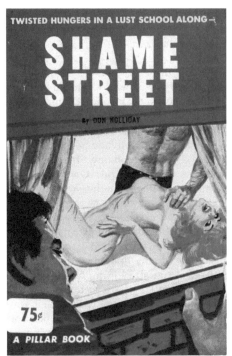

SHAME STREET

BY DON HOLLIDAY

75¢

A PILLAR BOOK

The word gets 'round and suddenly all the hookers in town want a piece of Don. At first, all this coupling has Don seeing stars, imagining an entire life of one night stands but, eventually, the young man decides that he really wants a steady girl to come live with him. Luckily, he runs into Mary, the girl recently dumped by he-man Ben Flake, and the two discuss and shake on a deal for mutual respect and long, lusty nights.

As for Ben, his weekend includes several sexual encounters, a few brushes with the law, watching his friend Tony Haze accidentally OD on pure heroin, and taking that first step to becoming *the* pimp on the block by asking Maybelle to move in with him. The close of the book finds Ben in a pensive move after sampling Maybelle's experience:

He butted the cigarette in the ashtray and turned away from the window as one last car rolled by forlornly in the night. A new week had begun, but there was no difference. Ben went back into the bedroom and crawled into bed with Maybelle. In her sleep she turned to him and he held her in his arms because it was warmer that way, and together they slept and the night went by and they would forget the weekends so that the years would pass, painlessly, because they were unremembered.

Shame Street is really nothing more than a series of vignettes, stitched together by trips back to the bar, but it's undeniably entertaining and the main characters are all fleshed out by interesting backstories and intriguing motivations. In plot and pace, I'd compare **Shame Street** to Clyde Allison's **The Lustful Ones** (actually written by William Knoles, and reviewed way back in issue one), without going so far as to say it's that novel's equal in the quality writing department. **Shame Street** seems to arrive at the point in the Greenleaf history where the "harder stuff" is starting to creep in. It's still all simply suggested or masked in subtle analogies but a couple of risqué passages manage to find their way in, such as in the sequence when Ben and some of his bowery boys proposition a young girl just out of Sunday sermon:

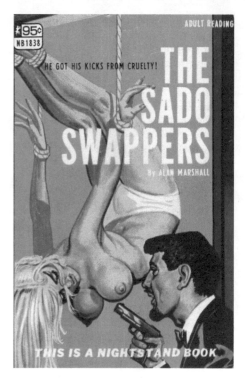

"Hey, I'll give you a dollar if you let us do it to you."

"Nope, I don't let boys do it to me."

"How about using your hand?"

"For a dollar?"

"Naw. Give you half a dollar for that."

She thought about it. He took out a half-dollar and flipped it, and it glinted in the sun.

"Okay," she said.

"Me first."

She went over to the wall and leaned against it and he went over and stood facing her. She reached out slowly and took him in her hand, caressing tentatively at first and then going faster as she got used to the rhythm. All the others crowded around to watch.

"Don't get me dirty," she said, sensing his readiness.

But he did.

He stepped away, smiling and fastening his clothes. Sue looked disgustedly at her Sunday dress and said, "Be more careful, huh?" to the next guy in line.

No, it's not quite *Penthouse Variations* (that would have to wait a few more years) but it's miles away from the PG-rated titillation of the Newsstand Library novels.

The Sado Swappers
by Alan Marshall (Harvey Hornwood)
Nightstand, June 1967
Cover Artist: Tomas Cannizarro
Sex: ★★★★
Story: ★★★
Cover: ★★★★

Jerry Werner is a man with a big problem. Though most of his S&M peccadillos are satisfied through his membership at an elite bondage group known as *The Club*, Jerry finds that he just can't get off when he knows the girls that are trussed up or tied down for his benefit every Friday night are 100% copasetic with their treatment. What he needs, his friend Larry insists, is to graduate to the big leagues:

"What you need," he went on, "is a club like the one used to be run by a chap I knew in Tangier before the war. Fantastic place. Cost a mint to get anywhere near it, but it was worth it. Great huge place it was. Once you go inside — if you got past the fellas at the door — you'd think you were in a sadist's paradise. If there is such a thing. Fabulous. Women everywhere.

Chap was a big la-de-da in the slave traffic, that sort of thing, and these women weren't willing, I can tell you. There were women hanging from the ceiling, women stretched along the walls, women chained to the tables. And all over were racks full of whips and lashes and canes and what have you. You just picked out whatever you liked and went to work. Remember once he had a girl swinging from the ceiling next to a little brazier with branding irons in it, with a little sign around her neck saying 'Burn me' in five languages. Sign wasn't necessary, of course. Needless to say, the place was always in a horrible uproar, all that screaming going on constantly. Girls got pretty mutilated, some of them, but there always seemed to be a fresh supply whenever one went back. Then there were women tied in kneeling positions — the men would just line up in front of them. Had a unique way of keeping track of your drink bill, too. Every man would be assigned a certain part of his waitress' body, and for each drink he had he'd burn a mark on her with a cigarette, and they'd add 'em up when he left. If you didn't happen to be smoking a cigarette at the time, the girl herself would light one up and hand it to you. Sold a lot of drinks that way, too. One of the greatest places I've ever seen, that was. 'Course there's no more like that nowadays. Good old Abdul." He sipped at his wine pensively.

The sadistic urge is distracting Jerry to such a point, he finds it impossible to work, sleep, or eat. He decides the only way he can find satisfaction is to *take* what he wants at any cost. Larry knows a guy who knows a guy who can set up a home invasion for Jerry. The family targeted includes a forty-ish mother with two daughters in their teens; dad will be out of town on business for the whole weekend. The catch, Larry explains, is that the three victims cannot be left alive to identify their assailants. Armed with handguns, Jerry and two thugs bust into the family's house and rape and sodomize the women over a span of eighty pages. No degradation is left unturned, no inch of skin left unblistered, as in a particularly grueling scene where one of the women is tossed into a shower of scalding water:

Howling now, Ann began to run frantically and aimlessly around the small rectangle, seeking a momentary escape from the pitiless stream. She made a strange, awkward figure, her hands behind her, her breasts bouncing, her feet slipping on the smooth floor. Jerry kept the powerful spray on her wherever she went, playing it up and down her body. Her screams reverberated through the tiled room.

Jones opened the door. Ann, still shrieking, crawled out of the stall on her knees. Her entire body was an angry red.

What to make of **The Sado Swappers**? I gotta tell you, I was not prepared for that final eighty pages, the equivalent of a 1980s Zebra horror paperback, and yet I couldn't put the damn thing down. I'm either a misogynistic pig or just incredibly curious. The tone shift halfway through is so stark it's as though author Harvey Hornwood decided the story of a weak man and his pursuit of love, amid his kinky desires, was one told too often in Greenleaf books. Damned if he wasn't going to make his readers sit up and take notice. Well, *I* noticed, Harvey.

Up to this point, I've stumbled on a few Greenleafs that were something more than just sex books, novels where it's clear the author is adding some steamy or semi-steamy interludes to ensure the sale of his manuscript. **The Sado Swappers** feels like something else entirely. There's a love for humiliation and perversion I've never encountered before in a novel (outside of, as noted, contemporary horror novels), especially one designed to titillate. Hornwood salivates over every scene of women licking dirty plates on their hands and knees and nipples burned by cigarettes. The "sex" scenes blend and interweave in a sensory overload in that final half of the book where Jerry and his boys check off their de Sade bucket list. It's amazing how, by 1967, how many restrictions were dropped from the "No No list." Oh, and **(SPOILER ALERT!)** there's no happy ending, no sudden revelation that the whole event was staged for Jerry's benefit. This is nasty shit. Shout out to readers: if you've read any sleaze more vile than this one, drop me a line.

The ideally named Hornwood wrote two other books for Greenleaf: **Lust Rumble** (Nightstand, January 1966) and **Passion's Pupil** (Pleasure Reader, January 1969). Both are priced well out of my reach at the moment, but I'll be hunting for some dog-eared copies. Hornwood wrote an essay on his Greenleaf days, and what he felt were the best of the sleaze writers, in the May 1990 issue of *Penthouse Forum* (and reprinted in Earl Kemp's essential online zine, eI, located at *efanzines.com*).

STOP THE PRESSES!

Last issue I ran reviews of books all featuring the same cover artist. At the time, I had no idea who the artist was (despite checking a half-dozen sources), but one of the bonuses of a public forum is that the writer (this one, at least) always seems to have an audience with pertinent information and a desire to share it. To the rescue comes writer Brian Emrich, frequent contributor to Gary Lovisi's *Paperback Parade*, who lets us know that the cover art was created by Oscar Liebman.

Brian points out that Liebman was a "prolific artist doing broadway playbill covers, album covers, mainstream paperback covers and hardcovers, men's adventure covers and interiors, you name it, he was a big player." Thanks very much to Brian for clearing up the mystery! Here are three more Liebman covers to enjoy!

Mexican Mantrap (Gaslight, 1964)

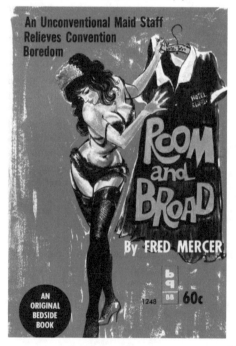

Sins of the Flesh (Gaslight, 1964)

Room and Broad (Bedside, 1963)

The word "novelization" has always been in the dictionary, meaning "to convert something into the form of a novel."

The usage has been around since the early 1800s, when it referred to transforming stage play narrative into books and was derided as "that queer, clumsy, mongrel species" by *The Nation*. By 1995, Randall Larson called it "a highly-misunderstood writing specialty."*

Novelizations or "tie-ins" are generally understood to mean a TV or movie shooting script, pumped up to fifteen times its original typographical density and arranged into arbitrary chapters by that bread-and-butter mercenary of literature, the Writer For Hire. Film novelizations go all the way back to the silents, even including *Les Vampires* (1915-16) and *London After Midnight* (1927). One of the most famous early ones based on a talkie was *King Kong* (1932), written by Delos W. Lovelace at the request of director Merian C. Cooper. Why? For publicity — as advertising to precede the 1933 release of the film. (It's fascinating to see that the book cover even credits scenarists James A. Creelman and Ruth Rose, although Cooper and Edgar Wallace get the biggest type.)

The real heyday of the novelization was the period immediately preceding the cultural tidal wave of home video. Why? Because if you were fond of a film, there existed very few collectibles or physical artifacts through which you could re-live the experience. You might be able to grab a one-sheet poster if you had the right theater connections. Of course, movie fan magazines offered the usual publicity pictures and little depth. There might be a comic book or an occasional toy spinoff. But there was none of the chaotic IP and franchise servicing that is commonplace today, the coldly-strategized floodtides of merch. A novelization — generally a paperback original, rarely a hardcover — was the *entire movie*, brought back for your personal enjoyment, and sometimes it even had pictures!

* **Films Into Books: An Analytical Bibliography of Film Novelizations, Movie, and TV Tie-Ins**, *(Scarecrow Press, 1995).*

In 1939, Pocket Books introduced America to the paperback — ten titles *"for which thousands of people have paid from $2 to $4,"* for only 25¢ each. (This splashy debut put *Wuthering Heights* — then almost a hundred years old — on the bestseller list.) One of the inaugural titles was a reprint of James Hilton's *Lost Horizon*, to tie in with Frank Capra's 1937 film. A cover painting depicted a scene from the movie, and the book sold over a hundred thousand copies. The lesson that special cover art could help vend many copies of any novel upon which a movie was based was not lost on all the competing publishing houses, and the boom was on.

Sometimes these reprints were called "movie editions."

The vogue peaked in 1959 for two reasons: the movie-crushing specter of television, and (what else?!) governmental scrutiny focused on the lurid paperback cover illustrations, many of which were deemed suggestively pornographic — smoking pistols, half-naked dames, bondage symbology, that sort of thing.

The psychology of the tie-in was devastatingly simple: A favorably-impressed filmgoer comes out of the theater both hungry for reinforcement and susceptible to a tangible souvenir of that pleasurable viewing experience, since anything derived from that is a fairly reliable proposition as entertainment. The logic was elemental: If a consumer was willing to lay down cash for a tie-in born of a film born of a novel, why not a "novel" born of a screenplay that didn't come from a book in the first place?

A few pages of philistine, hardcore, boilerplate contract-ese later, the novelization as we know it today was born. Often pseudonymous, generally cranked out in a rampant hurry to meet an impossibly immediate deadline at survival wages with no royalties or percentage, these books claimed the niche vacated by the fast-and-dirty pulp magazines and the hard-boilers of the classic Gold Medal era. Plenty of "respectable" writers saw no conflict in trading fast typing for ready cash (and plenty of them couldn't resist churning out "one-handers" for the likes of Nightstand books, either). Writers capable of producing 50,000 words in a week could keep themselves in coffee and cigarettes long enough to produce something more personal, if desired. Novelizations were also a completely accessible way to earn a living, and some writers such as Michael Avallone (the self-proclaimed "Fastest Typewriter in the East" with more than 180 books to his credit) came to specialize in them.

In my own case, I dabbled in many variants while aspiring to *all* of them. Ultimately I never did an outright movie novelization although I lobbied hard for a couple of Cronenberg films, and turned down offers for things like *Death Before Dishonor* (1987) and *Warlock* (1989). I remember hectoring Jon Davison for the opportunity to novelize *Gremlins* but lost out to George Gipe, who already had a track record and went on to do *Back to the Future* and *Explorers* (both 1985) as well. I also dipped a toe into the softcore realm before farming those titles out to an associate.*

I did this with a number of TV tie-ins, too, on behalf of a couple of friends who didn't mind being walked into their first (and frequently *only*) book credit, albeit pseudonymously. I'd secure the deal and sometimes write the first chapter or three, hand them a deadline and some cash, and *abracadabra!* Sometimes it actually worked out. Some other times it turned into a rescue operation. I felt a little bit like Charles Beaumont must have felt, parceling out magazine and *Twilight Zone* assignments to fellow members of the Green Hand or the Group. Why, again? Because after breaking the ice with a studio licensing department and delivering the goods to their satisfaction, they were offering me multi-book deals, sometimes for four books at once.

During the 1980s I wrote, launched, or oversaw nearly twenty books this way, almost all prior to my first published novel under my own name in 1987, although of

---

* Because in a field where the payday was three to five grand, for some obscure reason the per-book payout on those particular "stiffeners" was a deliriously irresistible $8500.

necessity there was a bit of overlap. For one series of books, I wrote more (published) entries than the person who created the series.

Then one day I was at Universal Studios and the licensing director for merchandising handed me a videotape and directed me to a vacant office where I watched the pilot for *Miami Vice*, about six weeks prior to its debut on NBC. The script by Anthony Yerkovich was vivid, muscular and cinematic. Would I care to write the novelization?

And another pseudonym was born. Welcome to the world, "Stephen Grave"!

This was 1985. I was still banging away mostly on a Smith-Corona manual portable typewriter. I wound up writing six *Miami Vice* paperbacks, mostly for publication in the UK via Star/Target Books. Only the first two were published Stateside, but they were slightly trimmed down from their UK versions. Nonetheless, they garnered favorable reviews. More to the point was that they garnered reviews *at all*, which almost never befell TV tie-ins. But *Miami Vice* quickly waxed into a global sensation; I received translations in Spanish, German, Japanese, Italian, French, Dutch, even *hardcover* versions in Hebrew!

Yes, I wrote them very quickly. Avallone would have been proud. My personal best for a 60,000-word manuscript was *four days*. (I had misinterpreted a deadline and didn't want to blow it. I had a weekend. That Saturday I typed 80 pages and fell asleep with my hands practically paralyzed. It was pure, hyper-caffeinated stream-of-consciousness writing with no review and no turning back. And yes, I made the deadline the following Monday.)

Historically, I was in fine company. Truly, anybody worth his or her writer-hat could bash out one of these things in a few weeks, thereby magnifying the available time for (1) other projects, or (2) goofing off. Novelizations tempted legitimate writers with a large, ready audience — film fans — and the dubious associations of the movie biz. (You'll find that many writers who ballyhoo themselves as *"New York Times Bestselling Authors"* achieved that bestselling status through the novelization

of a popular movie.) Further, there was the possibility that publishers might take you more seriously if they could see your byline on a continuing succession of paperbacks (another strategy I attempted to relentlessly exploit ... and which actually worked one single time, when I stacked a bunch of books on one executive's desk as my on-the-spot "resume.")

In the science fiction field, established names often adorned novelizations. The "W. J. Stuart" who did *Forbidden Planet* in 1956 was long rumored to be Jack Williamson (because of the "W.J.," reversed) but was actually mystery writer Phillip MacDonald. Rod Serling wrote his own *Twilight Zone* tie-in paperbacks. In 1966, Fritz Leiber did *Tarzan and the Valley of Gold*, which today is a collector's item of far more interest than the Mike Day film from which it derives. The same year, Isaac Asimov delivered *Fantastic Voyage* — his only novelization (naturally he was so dissatisfied with the "science" of this potboiler that he was inspired to write a lectorial sequel, *Fantastic Voyage II: Destination Brain* [1987]). With the visibility and success of his *Star Trek* novelizations, James Blish arguably became the father of the ceaseless floodtide of books, spinoffs, series and concordances that followed. The names of John Jakes, Jerry Pournelle, David Gerrold and George Alec Effinger can all be found on *Planet of the Apes* tie-ins (Avallone, too!); ditto Thomas Disch, Hank Stine and David McDaniel for *The Prisoner*. Arthur C. Clarke's *2001: A Space Odyssey* (1968) can technically be considered a novelization, since it expands on his short story "The Sentinel" in service of the film's release. Ben Bova did *THX-1138* (1971; "corrected" edition, 1978), Robert Bloch novelized *Twilight Zone: The Movie* in 1982, and Piers Anthony did the same for *Total Recall* in 1990.

Scholastic Press issued little-seen novelizations of such sci-fi movies as *The Day the Earth Stood Still* (by Arthur Tofte, 1976) and *Silent Running* (by Harlan Thompson, 1972).

Science fiction's prima facie case is the career of Alan Dean Foster, who broke through with a series of paperbacks based

on the *Star Trek* cartoon show and eventually cornered the market with novelizations for *Dark Star, Alien, Clash of the Titans, Outland, The Black Hole, The Thing, Krull,* and more. Reliable and prolific, Foster further qualified his foothold by authoring one of the biggest genre novelizations of all time. After the flat fee of $5000 offered by George Lucas was turned down by two other writers, Foster accepted the pseudonymous gig to write *Star Wars*. The paperback's bestselling status cemented his negotiating clout, which meant that all his future work would bear his real name. Foster's approved spinoff work, *Splinter of the Mind's Eye* (1978), proved as popular as nearly anything else with *Star Wars* stamped on its underbelly. (In the very rare cases where royalties were offered for novelizations, they generally fell in the 1-2% range.)

To the charge that novelizations were somehow "lowbrow" writing, Foster observed: "It's always amusing to me — you take a book, say, *To Kill a Mockingbird,* throw away three quarters of it and win an Academy Award for best adapted screenplay. But if you take a screenplay and add three quarters of original material to it — which is a much, much more difficult piece of writing — well, that's by definition 'hackwork.' And it's much harder, having done both, to take a screenplay and make a book out of it than [to] take a terrific book and make a screenplay out of it."*

When Disney bought Lucasfilm in 2012, they failed to meet their royalty obligations to Alan Dean Foster not only for the *Star Wars* and *Splinter of the Mind's Eye* books, but for the *Alien* novelizations (the first three movies) acquired via swallowing 20th Century-Fox in 2019. Rather brashly, Disney claimed to have purchased the rights, but not the obligations of the original deals. Foster took his case public in 2021, which brought down a PR catastrophe (the #*DisneyMustPay* Task Force) in which the litigious and megalithic Maus House was forced to yield not only to Foster, but to settle with Donald F. Glut (*The Empire Strikes Back*) and James Kahn (*Return of the Jedi*), as well.**

Leaving a lot of lower-tier writers *not* tied to the apron strings of blockbuster

---

* Quoted from "Yes, People Still Read Movie Novelizations … and Write Them, Too," by Alex Suskind (*Vanity Fair,* 27 August 2014).

** Foster makes no mention of his legal contretemps in his new book about novelizationializing, **The Director Should've Shot You,** *still available from Centipede Press although the signed editions are sold out. For the record, George Lucas granted him half of one percent on earned revenue.*

franchises at the bottom of a pit, staring up at their tormentors. For now.

I'm not a member of the International Association of Media Tie-in Writers, but I'm pleased it exists. Founded in 2006 by prolific wordsmiths Max Alan Collins and Lee Goldberg (and still going strong), the organization annually bestows the Scribe Awards, as well as the Faust Award for Lifetime Achievement.

Negative connotations are perpetual and tough to overcome; witness an article from the *Chicago Tribune*, "Movie Novels are Still Around, and They Aren't All Trash" (30 March 2020). (Nonetheless, the article does offer a beautiful image when it describes tie-ins as *"a marketing niche that once found its spiritual home in spinning wire racks at drugstores."*) Even the *Guardian*, eager to exploit the exception when Quentin Tarantino book-i-fied his own film, *Once Upon a Time in Hollywood*, couldn't resist summing up all those *other* novelizations as *"the lowliest kind of movie brand promotion; a genre the literary world wrinkles its nose at."*

George Lucas received cover credit for that *Star Wars* book, naturally, as did Steven Spielberg for *Close Encounters of the Third Kind* (1979), actually-written by Leslie Waller. Populist TV producer Glen Larson always took cover co-credit in first position, ahead of the novelizationist, for the authorship of things like the *Battlestar Galactica* series of paperbacks — books he never wrote or even saw, let alone read. Other novelizations are often more intriguing for who did *not* make the credit cut . . . or get involved at all. Stephen King turned down $25,000 — then a record for the field — to novelize *Poltergeist* (1982). Thereafter, Jeff Rovin wrote some 60 pages of copy for a cool ten grand before the project was passed on, at an equivalent rate, to Joe Haldeman. It finally wound up in the typewriter of James Kahn.

Ramsey Campbell wrote (and introduced) three titles in the "Universal Horror Library" in 1977: *The Bride of Frankenstein, Dracula's Daughter* and *The Wolf-Man*. He was credited as "Carl Dreadstone" in the US And "E.K. Leyton" in the UK. Ditto Walter Harris, who wrote for this same series *The Werewolf of London*,

Creature from the Black Lagoon and most likely *The Mummy*. Verification of Harris' authorship of *Creature* absorbed years of fan inquiry; the jury's still out on *The Mummy* although the most likely course would have been to divide the series between the two known writers.

And *Creature from the Black Lagoon* was novelized more than once — John Russell Fearn had first adapted it in 1954, as "Vargo Statten."

Other movies received multiple novelizations according to which side of the Atlantic you were on. Ron Goulart wrote *Capricorn One* (1978), but in England a novelization with different plot developments was written by bestselling author Ken Follett under the pseudonym "Bernard L. Ross." *Ghostbusters* (1984), the novelization done for the UK by Larry Milne, is far different from the book that appeared as *Ghostbusters: The Supernatural Spectacular* (1985) by Richard Mueller in the US. *The Terminator* (1984) was credited to Randall Frakes & Bill Wisher in the States, but gore specialist Shaun Hutson wrote the British version. *My Science Project* (1985) was novelized by Mike McQuay for the US, and Ian Don for the UK.

One of Philip K. Dick's final gestures was to refuse authorization of a book derived from the screenplay to *Blade Runner* (1982), which was based on his 1968 novel *Do Androids Dream of Electric Sheep?* Instead, the novel was reissued as a movie edition with Harrison's Ford's blandly-popular mug on the cover, and did as well as a new book cobbled from the script might have. This illustrates another odd trend when it comes to novelizations: the round-robin effect. Prior to *The Exorcist*, William Peter Blatty wrote a novel titled *Twinkle, Twinkle, "Killer" Kane* (1966), which he later directed as a film, *The Ninth Configuration* (1980). But before that he rewrote *Kane* into a new version, also titled *The Ninth Configuration* (1978), which he used to help sell the movie.

Another example that spanned decades began in 1938 with the publication of John W. Campbell's "Who Goes There?" in *Astounding Science Fiction* under the pseudonym Don A. Stuart. Twelve years later, the Charles Lederer screenplay for the Howard Hawks/RKO version of *The Thing from Another World* was "based on the story by Don A. Stuart.' In 1982, the Bill Lancaster script for the John Carpenter remake of the Hawks film credited neither Hawks nor Lederer, but was "based on the story 'Who Goes There?' by John W. Campbell, Jr." Then came — what else? — the Alan Dean Foster novelization, "based on a screenplay by Bill Lancaster." Nearly eighty years after the ice had first been broken, Campbell's *original* version of the story — six opening chapters longer — was published for the first time as *Frozen Hell* (2019).

Novelizations present another wrinkle when it comes to film canon, continuity, and retcon. Tie-in writers are frequently compelled to invent material that turns out to be contrary to last-minute changes wrought in a finished movie, for example. Or worse, the filmmakers aren't forthcoming with detail, leading Alan Dean Foster to describe the facehugger in *Alien* as having a huge eye in the middle of its back. Stronger examples — especially to movie historians — are found in the likes of Kahn's *Poltergeist* (where the middle hundred pages explains randomly-linked occurrences in the film), or Vonda McIntyre's *Star Trek II: The Wrath of Khan*, which attempts to flesh out the cardboard denizens of the film as actual, whole characters.

More often, such quibbles 'n bits can be found in the original script, shot for the film . . . and then deleted before release. Or fabricated from whole cloth to suck up another four manuscript pages, details that might stick in the craw of some too-enthusiastic fan and prompt hellacious protest (such as Newt's variant age or the number of wheels on a troop transport in *Aliens*). A corollary to this is the degree of auctorial control imposed on some novelizationists by the IP holders, hit lists of do's and don'ts that rendered the whole process a lot more grueling for some unfortunate writers, even as the cap wordage stretched its reach toward a marathon 90,000 words, or more. This has become particularly egregious for binge-watchable TV shows, where the licensing entities attempt to exert a degree of nitpicky remote control that just sucks all the potential joy out of the enterprise.

Continuity in *Star Wars*? That way lies Bedlam-level madness.

But the fact remains that novelizations, once upon a time, were the only piece of a movie you could take home with you.

A primordial version of this piece first appeared in Arēs *Magazine (WInter 1983) under the same title.*

Cimarron Street Books is pleased to bring you

The Works of
DAVID J. SCHOW

Wild Hairs
The award-winning collection of essays including the collected "Raving & Drooling" columns from *Fangoria* Magazine . . .

Crypt Orchids
Our edition features an introduction by and interview with Robert Bloch, an updated afterword, and a previously uncollected story, "The Mystery Buff."

Silver Scream
DJS's "best original anthology of the 1980s" features 20 stories from Barker, Bloch, Campbell, Lansdale, McCammon, Wilson and more . . .

Seeing Red
DJS's first collection, back in print with an all-new interview on *Rod Serling's Twilight Zone Magazine* and the state of horror publishing in the 1980s!

Monster Movies
An all-new collection of 13 of DJS's stories featuring many classic monsters, alongside "The Finger." With an Introduction by Greg Nicotero, and cover art by Reynold Brown!

Eye
For the first time in paperback, DJS's fifth collection is back in print with two all-new stories and a new cover and interior illustrations by Thomas Canty!

Zombie Jam
All of DJS's classic zombie fiction is collected in a single, expanded volume — 2x as much as the original edition — and fully illustrated by Bernie Wrightson!

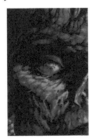

Weird Doom
What is *Weird Doom*? It's essentially a sampler of all of the above, with new commentary on the Cimarron Street Books' editions, and the first appearance of an all-new short story, "Caving."

Lost Angels
An all-new edition of DJS's second collection with an introduction by Richard Christian Matheson, an updated afterword, and the first paperback publication of his novella "Rock Breaks Scissors Cut."

For the latest updates, follow us on online at: CimarronStreetBooks.com

A GOOD CAST IS WORTH REPEATING

Stephen R. Bissette, a pioneer graduate of the Joe Kubert School, was an instructor at the Center for Cartoon Studies from 2005-2020. He is renowned for his work on *Swamp Thing*, *Taboo* (launching **From Hell** and **Lost Girls**), *1963*, *S.R. Bissette's Tyrant®*, co-creating John Constantine, and creating the world's second '24-Hour Comic' (invented by Scott McCloud for Bissette). Comics creator (*Spongebob Comics*, *Paleo*, *Awesome 'Possum*), illustrator (**Vermont Monster Guide**), author (**Teen Angels & New Mutants**, short fiction in **Hellboy: Odd Jobs, The New Dead, Mister October**, co-author of **Comic Book Rebels, Prince of Stories: The Many Worlds of Neil Gaiman, The Monster Book: Buffy the Vampire Slayer**), Bissette's latest includes the books **Cryptid Cinema**™, the 'Midnight Movie Monograph' **David Cronenberg's The Brood**, sketchbooks **Thoughtful Creatures** and **Brooding Creatures**, and co-authoring **Studio of Screams**. He also contributes bonus features and commentary tracks to Blu-rays & boxed sets from Arrow Video, Kino Lorber, Severin, Scorpion Releasing, and others.

Matthew R. Bradley is the author of **Richard Matheson on Screen: A History of the Filmed Works** (McFarland, 2010) and the co-editor, with Stanley Wiater and Paul Stuve, of **The Richard Matheson Companion** (Gauntlet, 2008). He is preparing a comprehensive screen history of the "California Sorcerers" writers' group that included Robert Bloch, Ray Bradbury, George Clayton Johnson, Matheson, William F. Nolan, Jerry Sohl (all of whom he interviewed extensively), and Charles Beaumont. He explores "the nexus of film and literature" at his blog, Bradley on Film (bradleyonfilm.wordpress.com).

J. Charles Burwell is a long-time reader and collector of vintage paperbacks and pulps. For over forty years, he has been both an aficionado and admittedly amateur scholar of Hardboiled, Noir, and Western fiction. Beginning with a tattered Dell Mapback edition of Dashiell Hammett's **Nightmare Town**, his collection expanded to include copies of *Black Mask, Manhunt*, and paperback originals published by Gold Medal and Lion. He also collects the paperback covers of Avati, Meltzoff, and Zuckerberg. Author of an as-yet unpublished hitch-hiking memoir, **Going East, Will Share Gas**, he is currently at work on a collection, **Strange Tales of the '70s**. He can be reached at zenoir@optonline.net

Peter Enfantino is the co-author of **The Manhunt Companion** (Stark House, 2021) and an obsessive collector of Mystery, Crime and Horror digests including *Alfred Hitchcock, Manhunt, Mike Shayne*, as well as the entire stable of Warren Magazines. He has written for all the major channels on the topics, including *Paperback Parade, Mystery Scene, The Digest Enthusiast, Paperback Fanatic, Monster Maniac, Men of Violence, Mystery File, Comic Effect*, and Peter Normanton's *From the Tomb*. He is currently working on an exhaustive critical guide to the Atlas Pre-Code Horror Comic Books. In his spare time, he writes with Jack Seabrook on DC War comics, the Warren Publishing phenomenon, and Batman in the 1980s. He Lives in Gilbert, Arizona.

Ken Mitchroney's film and television credits include director, live action director, head of story, director of photography, and storyboard artist on *Storks, The Lego Movie, The Ant Bully, Toy Story 2, Monsters Inc, Mighty Magiswords*, and more. His comic book work includes *Ren & Stimpy, Teenage Mutant Ninja Turtles Adventures, Myth Conceptions*, and *Space Ark*. He co-authored the science fiction novel **Fata Morgana** with Steven R. Boyett. Mitchroney is also a voice actor, with roles including Evil Emperor Zurg in Disneyland's Buzz Lightyear "Space Ranger Spin" ride, and most recently Mr. Pachydermus and other characters in Cartoon Network's *Mighty Magiswords* animated series. He is an official *Rat Fink* artist for the Ed "Big Daddy" Roth estate, and is official illustrator for the Oakland Athletics (he previously did the same for the Baltimore Orioles). He is currently involved with the restoration of the Ward Kimball collection of locomotives at the Southern California Railway Museum in Perris, California. He has been a professional stock-car driver and pinstriper, and restores and runs vintage locomotives. He lives and works in the San Francisco Bay Area and Los Angeles.

Kim Newman is an award-winning writer, critic, journalist and broadcaster who lives in London. He is a contributing editor to the UK film magazine *Empire*, and writes its popular monthly segment, "The Cult of Kim Newman." He also writes for assorted publications including *Video Watchdog* ('The Perfectionist's Guide to Fantastic Video'), *The Guardian*, and *Sight & Sound*. His horror novels and short stories have won a number of industry 'bests', including the Bram Stoker Award for Best Novel (for his best-selling **Anno Dracula**). Under the pen name Jack Yeovil, he wrote a series of entertaining dark fantasy novels set in the Warhammer universe, and a series of science fiction apocalyptic horror novels known as Dark Future. Kim also writes non-fiction books focused on popular culture, film, and television, including a comprehensive overview of the horror film industry, **Nightmare Movies: Forty Years of Fear** (Bloomsbury). You can keep up-to-date with Kim's events and writing at johnnyalucard.com. His next novel is **Something More Than Night** (due from Titan Books in November), which is about Raymond Chandler and Boris Karloff – and might have been called **Once Upon a Time in Hollywood** if the title hadn't been taken.

William Schoell is the author of eleven novels and twenty-one non-fiction books including **The Horror Comics** and **Creature Features**. His vintage horror novels are now available in new trade paperback editions from Encyclopocalypse Publications, and as e-books through Cemetery Dance. His most recent novel is **Monster World**. His movie blogs are Great Old Movies (greatoldmovies. blogspot.com) and B Movie Nightmare (bmovienightmare.blogspot.com).

David J. Schow is a multiple-award-winning West Coast writer. The latest of his ten novels is a hardboiled extravaganza called **The Big Crush** (2019). The newest of his eleven short story collections is a compendium titled **Monster Movies** (2020). He has been a contributor to Storm King Comics' **John Carpenter's Tales for a Halloween Night** since its very first issue. In 2021, Storm King began releasing his eight-issue series *John Carpenter's Tales of Science Fiction — "Hell."* DJS has written extensively for film (*The Crow, Leatherface: Texas Chainsaw Massacre III, The Hills Run Red*) and television (*Masters of Horror, Mob City, Creepshow's* "The Finger"). His nonfiction works include **The Art of Drew Struzan** (2010) and **The Outer Limits at 50** (2014). He can be seen on various DVDs as expert witness or documentarian on everything from *Creature from the Black Lagoon* to *Psycho* to *I, Robot*, not to mention the Rondo and Saturn Award-winning *Outer Limits* (Seasons 1 and 2) discs from Kino Lorber and Via Vision. Thanks to him, the word "splatterpunk" has been in the Oxford English Dictionary since 2002.

John Scoleri is the author of several books on artist Ralph McQuarrie, including **The Art of Ralph McQuarrie: ARCHIVES** (Dreams & Visions Press, 2015), and the producer of the DVDs *Ralph McQuarrie: Illustrator* (2002) and *Caroline Munro: First Lady of Fantasy* (2004). Publications under his Cimarron Street Books imprint include the works of David J. Schow, the magazine you're currently holding and the forthcoming **Raiders of the Lost Art: The Unseen Designs of Movie Tie-In Solicitation Covers**. He curates the **I Am Legend** Archive (iamlegendarchive.com) from his home in Santa Clara, California, where he is currently at work on **Latent Images** (Dreams & Visions Press), a photographic retrospective of George A. Romero's *Night of the Living Dead*.

Duane Swierczynski is the two-time Edgar-nominated author of ten novels including **Revolver**, **Canary**, and the Shamus Award-winning Charlie Hardie series. Duane has written various bestselling comics for Marvel, DC, Dark Horse, Archie and Valiant, including *Cable, Deadpool, The Immortal Iron Fist, Punisher MAX, Birds of Prey, Star Wars: Rogue One, Godzilla, Bloodshot* as well as his creator-owned *Breakneck* and most recently, *John Carpenter's Tales of Science Fiction — "Redhead."* Duane's short story "Lush" was included in **The Best American Mystery Stories 2019**, and he is currently adapting it into a feature film for Lionsgate. A native Philadelphian, he lives in Los Angeles with his family and attends double features at the New Beverly as often as possible.

S. Craig Zahler is an award-winning screenwriter, director, novelist, cinematographer, and musician. He wrote, directed, and co-composed the score for the 2015 film *Bone Tomahawk*, an Independent Spirit Award nominated picture (Best Screenplay; Best Supporting Actor) starring Kurt Russell. Zahler also wrote and directed *Brawl in Cell Block 99*, a *New York Times* Critic's Pick, starring Vince Vaughn. Both movies were added to the permanent collection of the Museum of Modern Art in New York City in 2017. Mel Gibson and Vince Vaughn star in Zahler's new crime drama *Dragged Across Concrete*. Zahler's debut Western novel, **A Congregation of Jackals** was nominated for the Peacemaker and the Spur awards, and his 2014 novels **Mean Business on North Ganson Street** and **Corpus Chrome, Inc.** both received starred reviews for excellence in *Booklist*. His book **Hug Chickenpenny: The Panegyric of an Anomalous Child** is a gothic tale will bring to the silver screen with the help of his new creative partners, The Jim Henson Company. After reading this strange story, Clive Baker declared, "S. Craig Zahler is certain to become one of the great imaginers of our time." His latest novel is **The Slanted Gutter**.

back•issues

TSF #1 - SOLD OUT   TSF #2 - SOLD OUT   TSF #3 - $15

TSF #7 - $10   TSF #8 - SOLD OUT   TSF #9 - SOLD OUT

TSF #13 - SOLD OUT   TSF #14 - $18   TSF #15 - SOLD OUT

TSF #19 - $20

NOTLD - SOLD OUT

BB #1 - $10

Supplies are limited. Prices do not include shipping.

TSF #4 - SOLD OUT   TSF #5 - $7   TSF #6 - SOLD OUT

TSF #10 - $15   TSF #11 - $15   TSF #12 - $25

TSF #16 - $18   TSF #17 - $18   TSF #18 - $13

BB #2 - $10
(2020 Reprint)

BB #3/4 - $10
Magazine-Sized
Double Issue

BB #5 - $10
(2020 Reprint)

BB #6 - $10

For ordering information, contact: CimarronStreetBooks@gmail.com

It's not too late to catch up on the best of *The Scream Factory* (1988-1997) or the original *bare•bones* (1997-2001)

From 1988-1997, *The Scream Factory* provided an exhaustive and often irreverent overview of all aspects of horror—from fiction to film and beyond. It became a go-to reference for horror aficionados around the globe. 20 years after the magazine ceased publication, the editors have sifted through the contents of the magazine's 20-issue run to assemble this 590-page 8.5″ x 11″ epic collection.

The Best of The Scream Factory ($29.95 TPB) reprints more than 70 articles from the magazine's golden age, covering such diverse topics as: the best horror novels of the '80s; a viewer's guide to Godzilla movies; horror in the pulps; the worst in horror; dark suspense fiction; the influence of *Night of the Living Dead* on fiction and film; horror on old-time radio; sci-fi/horror hybrids; Western horror; werewolf fiction; British horror fiction and films; Canadian horrors; and horror in the comics. In addition to the nearly 600-page selection of "greatest hits," the editors have penned a brand new 25,000 word introduction!

Born from the ashes of *The Scream Factory*, *bare•bones* (1997-2001) unearthed some of the best vintage and forgotten paperbacks, films, pulp fiction, television, and video. *bare•bones — the best of —* ($16.95 TPB/$22.95 HC) collects many of the best articles from the magazine's original run, including:
 • Overviews of fiction series including: George Chesbro's Mongo, Robert Lory's Dracula, Richard Stark's Parker, John Sanford's Prey novels, Karl Edward Wagner's Kane, and the Black novels of Cornell Woolrich!
 • Retrospectives on filmmakers Edward L. Cahn and Jerry Warren!
 • An overview of the Blind Dead films!
 • Ann-Margret movie tie-ins!
 • Annotated Indexes to *Saturn Science Fiction* and *Web Detective Stories*!
 • A detailed overview of the *Dark Shadows* novels of Dan (Marilyn) Ross!
 • Commentary on Trevanian and Top Ten lists by David J. Schow!
 • A look back at the *Trilogy of Terror* Zuni!
 • Interviews with Bill Crider, Richard Prather, Robert Serling and Bay Area *Creature Features* horror host Bob Wilkins!

Order today on Amazon, eBay or through CimarronStreetBooks@gmail.com!

Made in United States
Troutdale, OR
11/30/2023